GW01605370

Alan Henry

HAZLETON PUBLISHING

250 GRAND PRIX

YEAR

WINS 1965-1991

PUBLISHER
Richard Poulter

EXECUTIVE PUBLISHER
Elizabeth Le Breton

ART EDITOR
Steve Small

PRODUCTION MANAGER
George Greenfield

HOUSE EDITOR
Peter Lovering

PRODUCTION ASSISTANT
Deirdre Fenney

STATISTICS
Jocelyne Bia

This first edition published in 1991 by Hazleton Publishing, 3 Richmond Hill, Richmond, Surrey TW10 6RE.

ISBN: 0-905138-84-8

Printed in England by Richard Clay Ltd, Bungay, Suffolk.

Typeset by First impression, Richmond, Surrey.

Colour reproduction by Adroit Photo Litho Ltd, Birmingham.

DISTRIBUTORS

UK & OTHER MARKETS
George Philip Ltd
59 Grosvenor Street
London W1X 9DA

NORTH AMERICA
Motorbooks International
PO Box 2
729 Prospect Avenue
Osceola
Wisconsin 54020, USA

AUSTRALIA
Technical Book & Magazine Co. Pty
289-299 Swanston Street
Melbourne
Victoria 3000

Universal Motor Publications
c/o Automoto Motoring Bookshop
152-154 Clarence Street
Sydney 2000
New South Wales

NEW ZEALAND
David Bateman Ltd
PO Box 65062
Mairangi Bay
Auckland 10

PHOTOGRAPHS CONTRIBUTED BY

THE GOODYEAR TIRE &
RUBBER COMPANY ARCHIVE

BERNARD CAHIER
PAUL-HENRI CAHIER
CHARLES BRISCOE-KNIGHT
DAVID PHIPPS

OTHER CONTRIBUTIONS BY

PHIPPS PHOTOGRAPHIC
SNOWDON & ASSOCIATES
SUTTON PHOTOGRAPHIC

Contents

Foreword

AYRTON SENNA

Goodyear's success in winning 250 Grands Prix relies on an ability to provide a reliable product which combines competitive performance with consistency and safety. Matched with these key elements is Goodyear's application to developing tyre technology which has seen them constantly improving standards – putting them at the forefront of racing and road car tyre performance.

My own association with Goodyear in Grand Prix racing has produced some notable personal landmarks; my first pole position and first race victory were on Goodyear rubber, and since then my two World Championships and all 28 of my Grand Prix victories have been achieved with the company's product. Throughout countless numbers of testing and racing miles my association with Goodyear and its technicians has developed to the point where I have tremendous confidence and respect for their achievements.

In a sport where results count for so much, Goodyear's record speaks for itself.

WORLD
CHAMPIONSHIP
DO BRASIL
Beba
Guaraná
ANTARCTICA
Shell
MOËT & CHANDON
1
3

Preface

LEO MEHL

This book is dedicated to the thousands of Goodyear personnel worldwide who are the real hidden heroes of our 250 victories. Those of us mentioned in the book have enjoyed the thrill of victory and the agony of defeat, but the real winners are all those who made key contributions but never got any direct reward, except to know the World Championship or the win at Monaco wouldn't have happened without their efforts.

Those who designed and compounded the tyres, or designed, drew or cut the moulds, or handled the most cantankerous tread compounds ever conceived by man; those who modified all of our equipment, or over the years built thousands of experimental test tyres, two at a time, few of which ever raced; those whose regular production schedules we disrupted; those who responded night and day to our endless shipping problems; those who mounted and balanced the tyres all over the world in all kinds of weather, jet-lagged and tired; those who paid the bills, unscrambled the accounting or typed the letters – they are the real heroes.

In summary, our unmatched record in Formula 1 is due to only one factor, people. Our racing staff over the years has been the best: great engineers and innovators; patient, persistent, talented production people who daily do things which they have never done before; and field personnel who are truly the most experienced and knowledgeable in the sport.

All this has been made possible by a Goodyear top management with a fierce desire to win.

Today, it's hard to realise how many races we lost in those early days. It took years to develop the technology to attract winning teams. Our losses just made management want to win more. To win, you've got to experiment and you've got to go fast. Sometimes we've made mistakes, and of course, when we have, it's been on worldwide television. So our management has had to answer some tough questions for us on many occasions. They stayed behind us and the results are 250 wonderful victories.

So I join our World Champions, Sir Jack Brabham, Denny Hulme, Jackie Stewart, Emerson Fittipaldi, Niki Lauda, James Hunt, Mario Andretti, Alan Jones, Keke Rosberg, Alain Prost, Nelson Piquet and Ayrton Senna, in saluting the Goodyearites who made it all possible.

Leo Mehl
Akron
Ohio
March 1991

GOODYEAR
250
GRAND PRIX WINS

The

1

Background to Racing

Maximum exposure. The Goodyear blimp has become a familiar sight at Grands Prix over the years.

The efforts which were responsible for propelling Goodyear to the height of international success and led to it achieving the historic milestone of 250 Grand Prix victories had their roots in the company's realisation, some thirty years ago, that it required a dramatic change of image.

In the mid-1950s, it commissioned a market survey which revealed that the publicly perceived Goodyear image was that of a rather conservative, staid and trusty American corporation. There was nothing wrong with that as such but, as Goodyear Director of International Racing Leo Mehl explains, it was an image that needed polishing considerably if the company was to expand its market share in the years that were to follow.

'The average Goodyear customer at the time was over fifty years of age, lived in a rural area and had an annual income of less than $10,000,' he recalls. 'We were regarded as an ultra-conservative and technically rather backward operation, so it didn't take a great deal of figuring out where we were going to be in another twenty years. As a result, the company decided to start the Goodyear "blimp" airship programme, for promotional purposes, and the racing programme to enhance both its image and technical knowledge.' Thus, in 1956, Goodyear set up its racing division to develop world land speed record tyres for Mickey Thompson and stock car racing tyres for NASCAR competition.

Goodyear had been founded in 1898 by Frank Seiberling in Akron, Ohio. He named the company 'Goodyear' in honour of Charles Goodyear who, nearly 60 years earlier, had discovered 'vulcanisation', the process by which sulphur is added to rubber to make it more useable.

While Charlie Mertz used Goodyear tyres on his Stutz to finish third in the third running of the Indy 500 in 1913, it wasn't until six years later that the world's largest tyre and rubber company got really serious about the world's largest motor race. A major development effort by Goodyear engineers produced tyres that helped drivers break the 100 mph barrier at the Brickyard in 1919.

Howdy Wilcox, who qualified his Peugeot at 101.01 mph, won that race at an average speed of 88.05 mph. Nine of the top ten finishers were on Goodyear rubber, and two went the distance without a tyre change – an almost unbelievable feat at the time.

After proving its technologically advanced Goodyear Cord tyres at

Left: **The imposing entrance to the Goodyear Tire and Rubber Company's headquarters in Akron, Ohio. Behind this façade, executives pondered the survey which revealed that the company had an ultra-conservative image, the survey which sowed the seeds of its racing involvement.**

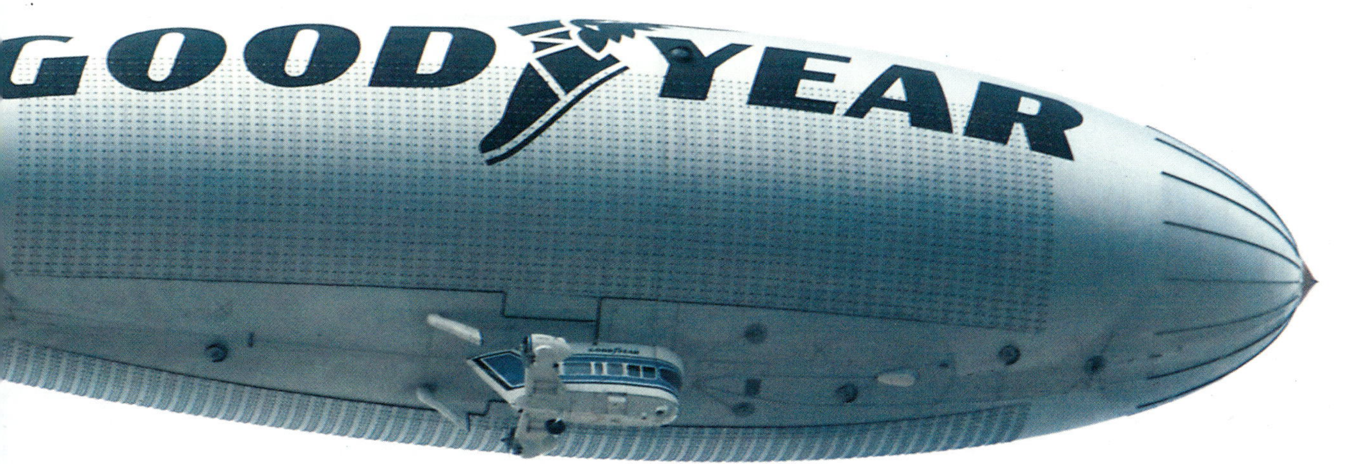

Chuck Daigh scrambles round Spa in the front-engined Scarab F1 car during practice for the 1960 Belgian Grand Prix. These machines took Goodyear rubber into the Grand Prix arena, albeit fleetingly, for the first time. But the Scarabs were outdated and ineffective even before their debut.

Indianapolis, the company reduced its racing involvement over the next few years and, in 1922, dropped out of active racing participation.

When the decision was made to return in the mid-1950s, Goodyear's preliminary forays into racing were made on a family of RR1 tyres, designed primarily for sports car use, using narrow, all-weather tread patterns. As Goodyear dabbled at tracks such as Daytona and Sebring during those early years, so the RR1 covers were modified and developed to provide a 'semi-slick' tread pattern for the stock cars, and this family of tyres endured for about five years.

During this period Goodyear made a preliminary, almost unnoticed foray onto the Grand Prix scene. In 1960 Lance Reventlow, millionaire son of Woolworth heiress Barbara Hutton, used Akron's products for his lavish and over ambitious F1 Scarab project. This proved a total failure.

Although Goodyear had entered the NASCAR arena in 1958, its first international racing foray was to Indianapolis in 1963, the result of an approach from 1961 winner A.J. Foyt. The Texan driving star was frustrated that Firestone had produced some special tyres for the trend-setting new rear-engined Lotus-Fords, to be driven by Jimmy Clark and Dan Gurney, but declined to supply any for his front-engined, Offenhauser-powered roadster. Satisfied with the performance of Goodyear tyres on his NASCAR stock saloon and AC Cobra sports cars, he approached Akron for a set of NASCAR tyres and they were duly despatched to the Brickyard.

After this preliminary test, Goodyear returned the following year with the purpose-made, 7-inch wide 'Goodyear Blue Streak Speedway Special'. Initially some 14 cars were equipped with this rubber, including Foyt, but when Parnelli Jones emerged with a special set of Firestones and an equally special qualifying engine to record a time some 5 mph faster than the Texan's, there was a wholesale switch back to the rival rubber. 'As things turned out, Foyt went on to win the race using Firestone tyres, but wearing his Goodyear driving suit!' explains Mehl with a twinkle in his eye.

Nevertheless, Goodyear would be back again with more suitable compounds for 1965, and two years later, with 16 starters on its tyres, Foyt sped to victory with his Goodyear-shod Coyote, registering the company's first Indy 500 victory in over four decades. In 1968, with 19 starters

Technicians checking the Goodyear race tyres on one of the works Brabham-Hondas which set the pace in Formula 2 during the 1966 season.

on Goodyears, Bobby Unser made it two wins in a row for Akron.

During the next three years the Indy 500 was won on Firestone tyres before Mark Donohue started Goodyear's domination that continues to this day by winning the Memorial Day classic in his Penske team McLaren-Offy.

Goodyear tyres were next raced in Europe on a single-seater car on 5 April 1964 when Frank Gardner used them on a John Willment-entered Lotus 27 at Pau, the street circuit in south-west France. It was an unsuccessful debut, for the rugged Australian finished this outing against an unyielding brick wall, after 'going great guns' according to Denis Jenkinson in *Motor Sport* magazine. Gardner would subsequently use Goodyears to great effect to win the British Saloon Car Championship on two occasions.

After testing the ground in 1964, Goodyear made a concerted effort in Grand Prix racing the following season, equipping the Brabhams of Dan Gurney and Jack Brabham and the works Hondas, and scored its first World Championship win when the late Richie Ginther took one of the Japanese machines to victory in Mexico.

The Goodyear International Corporation Racing Division established

Richie Ginther at the wheel of the 1½-litre Honda V12, scoring Goodyear's first Grand Prix victory at Mexico City, 1965.

Barry Griffin: currently Racing PR Manager and a Goodyear stalwart for many years.

Fred Gamble raced himself before playing a key role in establishing Goodyear's racing division at Bushbury, Wolverhampton in 1964.

its British base at Bushbury, Wolverhampton, where production began on 10 October 1964 with Fred Gamble as manager and Walt deVinney as Chief Engineer. They were two key personalities in the development of the company's racing heritage.

Gamble had briefly been a member of the Camoradi F1 team and actually raced in the 1960 Italian Grand Prix at the wheel of its Behra-Porsche special. DeVinney is still with the company as director of Goodyear's worldwide testing, responsible for all test tracks, fleets of cars and laboratories across the globe. Fred, however, would later quit corporate life and now runs a ski lodge in Snowmass, Aspen, Colorado. Prior to that he pursued a life of delivering yachts, surfing, writing and generally seeing the world. 'It's too bad we're not all as smart as Fred!' muses Leo Mehl.

Another early recruit to the racing division was Barry Griffin, who had joined Goodyear straight from national service in the RAF back in 1958. He moved to racing as office manager in 1966, enjoying a spell away in the automotive engineering department between 1971 and '79, before returning to become Manager of the European Race Tyre Division. Since 1984 he has fulfilled the valuable role of Racing PR Manager.

The Wolverhampton plant itself played a large part in Goodyear's history, the first brick being laid to build the British facility as long ago as 1927. Aircraft tyres were manufactured at Bushbury from 1930, with extensive factory expansion taking place over the years to the point where, by the mid-1960s, the total facility extended over an area of more than 100 acres.

Tyre designer Bert Baldwin, mould designer Don Moule and compounder John Shackleton were recruited from the British company before being sent to Akron for a training course, while Doug Nicholls was appointed Production Manager. In 1967 Shackleton moved to Akron and Sam Apticar came to England as Chief Compounder. Later that year Leo Mehl arrived to take over as racing manager, Fred Gamble moving to assume responsibility for Goodyear product sales in New Zealand.

Mehl was to become one of the key figures in Goodyear's Grand Prix involvement over the next quarter-century. Aged 32 at the time of his arrival in Europe, he briefly worked for Goodyear before serving three

Left: **Goodyear tyre engineer Bert Baldwin in conversation with Jack Brabham, the man who won the company's first World Championship in 1966.**

Goodyear's Director of International Racing is Leo Mehl ***(below)*****, one of the key proponents of the programme which led to those 250 Grand Prix victories.**

years in the US Air Force. On his return to the company in Akron, his career progress was quickly channelled into the chemical side of the race development programme.

Following a year in the laboratories, he was sent out on field work for the racing division, first working in NASCAR and then on the Shelby Cobra sports cars. He briefly became involved in Grand Prix racing during 1964 when the company did some testing with Jack Brabham in order to evaluate whether Goodyear could break into Formula 1. In 1964 and '65 he also came to Le Mans as part of the tyre support programme working with the Ford GT40 project, but subsequently switched to the all-important Indianapolis programme as a tyre compounder until late 1967, when he was chosen to come to Europe on a long-term basis.

His initial impression of the European F1 scene was that the competing

GOODYEAR WINS!

British Grand Prix

Brands Hatch, July 16th, 1966

1st JACK BRABHAM
driving a Brabham-Repco

2nd DENIS HULME
also driving a Brabham-Repco

3rd GRAHAM HILL
driving a B.R.M.

Results subject to official confirmation

This outstanding performance is yet another victory for Goodyear. It proves again that Goodyear tyres are unbeatable for strength, safety and stamina.

The same Goodyear know-how that produces the superb tyres for competitive driving makes possible the Goodyear tyres for your everyday motoring. They are both built with the same exclusive 3T cord and Tufsyn rubber. Racing and rally drivers depend on Goodyear tyres–*and so can you.*

Goodyear win the big ones! 1966 successes include:

Daytona 24-hour (USA) Feb. 5/6 · Sebring 12-hour (USA) Mar. 26 · Silverstone International Trophy Race May 14 Brands Hatch 500-mile (GT) May 8 · Le Mans 24-hour June 18/19 · French Grand Prix (European G.P.) July 3

Above left: **Linking racing achievements with the road-going product has always been one of Goodyear's prime advertisement priorities. Here Jack Brabham extols the virtues of its G800 radials. Goodyear's 1966 Le Mans 1-2-3 offered tremendous promotional benefits to the Akron company** *(above)*, **while Brabham's success in the British Grand Prix that year was represented by an illustration** *(opposite)* **typical of the period.**

teams were much more professional in their approach to the business than those he had experienced in the USA. On the other hand, he was surprised at just how amateur and disorganised the administration turned out to be at some of the races.

At Monaco in 1971, for example, the F1 tyre companies suffered considerable aggravation from the organisers, who only wanted to issue them with three tickets per company. Consequently, both Goodyear and Firestone threatened to pack up and leave, a ruse which prised another three passes apiece from the reluctant organisers. It wasn't enough, mind you, but it did represent a minor victory...

For 1966, Goodyear F1 contracts were signed with Gurney's new Eagle team in addition to Brabham, but it was Jack Brabham who dominated the scene, winning the French, British, Dutch and German Grands Prix to give Goodyear its first World Championship. Concurrently, Brabham and his team-mate, New Zealander Denny Hulme, notched up a total of 13 Formula 2 wins in their Goodyear-shod Brabham-Hondas.

The partnership with Brabham produced a second World Championship in 1967, this time with Hulme in the driver's seat, and the massive square-shouldered tyres, produced by the Bushbury design team led by Walt deVinney, provided the vital interface between car and track throughout this season.

Periodically, from 1975 to '77 and in 1987–88, Goodyear has found

Goodyear always prefers to battle against a rival tyre company in F1 rather than presiding over a monopoly situation. Here Alan Jones's Goodyear-shod Williams FW07 battles with Michelin user Gilles Villeneuve's Ferrari 312T4 for the lead of the 1979 Canadian Grand Prix at Montreal.

itself as a monopoly supplier to the front-line Grand Prix teams, yet Leo Mehl, who assumed the role of Director of International Racing in 1979, is absolutely clear in his mind that Goodyear's interests are best served by rivalry out on the circuits.

'We much prefer a fight, to be honest,' he explains, 'because the benefits in this business are pretty well split 50/50 between the advertising benefit and the technical feedback. But you run the danger of losing both benefits to some extent if you don't have the stimulus of competition. If you have a monopoly, for example, there is the ever-present danger that technical development may slow down slightly.'

Referring to the 1985 season, when Goodyear was battling hard against an emerging threat from Pirelli, he made the point that 'at the present time we do something in the order of ten major tyre tests every year, and every one of those is as intense and demanding as a racing event. That would be one area in which we would automatically cut back if we were on our own.

'From the publicity point of view, if you're in a monopoly situation

you also run the risk of bad publicity. The only way you get your name in the paper when you've got a monopoly is when you do something dumb. You read things like "he blew a tyre going into the first corner" or "the tyres were out of balance, so he stopped" or "it's too cold, so the tyres won't work" – I mean, how many times have you heard that one?

'So you really expose yourself and suddenly find that you haven't simply got five teams telling you what's wrong, but 25. And you've got nothing else left in the truck to give them as an alternative. That's the problem!'

Mehl emphasises that the technical challenge of F1 is so overwhelmingly demanding that one cannot sit back in a monopoly position and deal out any old tyre: 'You can't just make 15,000 covers and say to competitors, "Drop by the local warehouse and pick them up," because, if you do that, the chances are you'll be beaten by anybody – Avon, Pirelli, Bridgestone...anybody.

'You've got to tailor your tyres to suit the circuit, as much as anything for your own self-protection. Here I'm talking in terms of the safety of

Jackie Stewart was one of Goodyear's most respected ambassadors for almost twenty years.

the drivers at the same time as producing a tyre which is more than adequate for the race. You wouldn't want to risk ruining a race, for example, by saying, "Here's a nice hard rain tyre; this set will last you all season," and then find, when it rains for the first time, that they all crash.

'We've had a lot of experience about the possible pitfalls of this sort of situation with NASCAR. We had a NASCAR tyre supply monopoly for over ten years between the mid-1970s and mid-1980s, but we still provided something like fifteen different compound/constructions for the thirty or so events on the schedule. OK, like Indy car racing – and unlike F1 – it was a control tyre formula in the sense that the competitors didn't have any choice, but I've been in some pretty unpleasant situations where a control tyre has been used, perhaps into the following season, just to empty the warehouse.

'It is important if you are going to be in this business to do as good a technical job as you possibly can. If you take an unacceptably hard tyre to certain sorts of circuits, and you wind up by upsetting all your teams, it's probably better not to be there at all if you're not going to do the job correctly. And doing the job correctly is not influenced by whether or not you are operating in a monopoly situation.

'Of course, sometimes we encounter an element of opposition within the company which might say, "Why are you still involved when all we're doing is beating ourselves?" but this attitude is only valid if you have stopped developing the product. It might be right if you have stopped and are not contributing any longer, but we've learned that we'd better not stop contributing.

'As an example of that, we had a monopoly at Indy in the mid-1980s but that did not stop us converting to radial tyres because it was important for us to get radials into that high-speed arena and learn what there was to learn.'

One of Mehl's most spectacular successes was acquiring the services of Jackie Stewart and Tyrrell in time for the 1971 season. When Dunlop withdrew at the end of 1970, there was obviously considerable competition between Goodyear and Firestone to forge a deal with F1's pace-setting partnership. In fact, Mehl courted Stewart even before Dunlop's withdrawal, realising that the eloquent Scot could offer Akron many

Opposite: **Celebration of Jackie Stewart's second World Championship in 1971. This family shot in the paddock at Monza features Goodyear and Tyrrell racing personnel, those immediately surrounding the car including Jackie, designer Derek Gardner, Ken Tyrrell and François Cevert.**

RACING
TYRES
GOODYEAR
GOODYEAR
elf
30
GOODYEAR

Jackie Stewart and the Tyrrell-Ford, a partnership that won the World Championship on Goodyears in 1971 and '73. They also helped set the parameters for F1 tyre testing which exist to this day.

more advantages than simply his competitive ability out on the circuit.

'He was a marvellous ambassador, not only from the public relations viewpoint, but for the fact that he was ideal to explain to the top management just what benefits could accrue from an F1 racing programme,' Leo explains. 'Because Jackie was a household name, whose success was so well publicised, all the company employees, right down to the shop-floor level, could identify with him and feel that they played a part in his success.'

Stewart's relationship with Goodyear, both from a promotional and a technical development standpoint, endured for many years after the Scot's retirement from the cockpit in 1973. Continuing in that vein, Goodyear continued to forge and sustain links with the top drivers and teams over the next two decades, lending its support to the Formula 1 World Championship with a consistency of commitment that has now endured for a generation.

While commercial considerations necessarily govern the manner in which the company tackles its Grand Prix racing programme, Goodyear has demonstrated considerable operational resilience over the years. It has tried hard never to leave the Grand Prix scene in a situation where the finger of blame can be pointed in its direction in the event of an overall supply shortfall. That is a task that has not always been easy, particularly during the winter of 1986/87 when the company was subjected to a hostile takeover bid on the US stock market.

Nevertheless, Goodyear has a proven track record which points to continued, long-term involvement in Formula 1. Its success in achieving a record 250 Grand Prix victories bears witness to a sustained belief that motor racing provides not only a highly visible promotional medium, but also a competitive technical challenge of considerable and enduring value which would be impossible to reproduce in an artificial environment.

GOODYEAR

250

GRAND PRIX WINS

Goodyear's Grand Prix

2

Weekend

GOODYEAR
EAGLE
FONDMETAL

It is all too easy to take for granted the fact that a field of Grand Prix cars will roll out onto the circuit with metronomic dependability on 16 occasions during the battle for the World Championship. Whether the venue is Silverstone or Suzuka, Budapest or Brazil, the ongoing contest in motor racing's premier international league is organised with meticulous precision and timing. Yet the logistical challenge of moving huge mountains of equipment around the world is simply awesome, a task in which short-term improvisation and quick thinking can often prove as crucial as secure long-term planning.

As far as Goodyear's tyre supply facilities are concerned, the route from the source of manufacture in Akron, Ohio to the Grand Prix paddocks of the world can be lengthy and convoluted, depending on whether the races are taking place in Europe or further afield. The three races on the North American continent – Phoenix, Montreal and Mexico City – can be supplied by transporters directly from Akron, the European events by the European racing division at Bushbury, while those in other parts of the world rely on complex air charter arrangements in addition to collaboration with the local affiliate company in the country concerned.

Although organising air freight across the Atlantic poses few problems, it is an extremely expensive luxury, and Goodyear's budgets would take a severe hammering if this method were used regularly to deliver the 2400 or so tyres required for each Grand Prix weekend. Consequently, the company tries to organise its programme so that the bulk of the race tyre consignment is sent by sea freight, an exercise which generally takes about ten days from Akron to Bushbury.

Only if production falls behind schedule will the air freight option be employed for the final batch, and these late shipments are usually collected from Heathrow by one of the British transporters *en route* to the ferry. Air freight reduces the shipment time to around two days, door to door.

Goodyear's racing division has four of its own articulated transporters operating out of Bushbury, one of which is equipped as a service vehicle containing all the ancillary tackle needed to operate in the field – such as fitting and balancing equipment – in addition to carrying a reduced tyre load. However, as Operations Manager Tony Shakespeare

There is such a premium on space in the paddock at today's Grands Prix that the positioning of the transporters and motorhomes is a feat of planning in itself.

explains, this is not always sufficient to transport the requisite number of covers and additional transporters sometimes have to be hired for the job.

'In 1990, for example, we usually had six or seven articulated trucks servicing the European races,' he explains. 'That included our own four, plus another three on hire. Our drivers obviously have Heavy Goods Vehicle licences and generally double up as fitters, so we're talking in terms of 15 or 16 fitters in all. They take the vehicles to the track and, in addition, we send a smaller crew bus which leaves base along with the main fleet and carries any members of the team who don't possess HGV licences.'

For most European races, the Goodyear armada leaves Bushbury on Sunday or Monday night, drops into Heathrow if necessary to collect the final batch of tyres, then heads off to arrive in the Grand Prix paddock concerned by lunchtime on Wednesday. Setting up the Goodyear enclave in the paddock takes the rest of that day, assuming there are no unexpected snags or difficulties. In reality, such hiccups seldom occur. The Formula One Constructors' Association has evolved a system of laying out the F1 paddock with meticulous precision, all transporters and motorhomes fitting in neatly like a well-ordered jigsaw puzzle. As far as Goodyear is concerned, the priority is to be ready first thing on Thursday morning for the serious business of tyre fitting.

Wheel balancing must be carried out with meticulous precision; Senna and Prost won't be happy with wheel vibration at 170 mph!

The Goodyear personnel generally try to arrive in the paddock by 8.00 a.m. on Thursday morning. The tyre men from the individual teams will bring over their wheels after being given the allocation sheets for their cars, indicating the quantity of tyres available to them. Work on fitting the tyres generally starts at 9.00 a.m. and, by the time the day is over, between 600 and 650 tyres will have been fitted and balanced. It is quite demanding physical toil for those involved, but follows a well-practised format. Everybody in the Goodyear force knows what is expected of him and the operation generally runs with undramatic efficiency.

The first untimed session on Friday morning sees competitors checking the chassis set-up of their cars and not really chasing fast times. Towards the end of this 90-minute stint some of the drivers may switch to the soft-compound qualifying covers for a few laps, preparing themselves for the first hour-long qualifying session which is always scheduled between 13.00 and 14.00. After the untimed session, the team engineers will make a decision as to which tyres they will use for the first qualifying session and a flurry of activity follows during the 90 minutes which separate the two sessions as final choices are fitted to the rims.

Opposite: **Ferrari's tyre supply awaits.**

GOODYEAR
GOODYEAR
28
MAGNETI MARELLI
WEBER
EAGLE
EAGLE
4699
SET. 14
SPEEDLINE

Whether it is Monza in the Seventies ***(inset)*** **or Phoenix in the Nineties, Goodyear fitters reckon to mount in the region of 600 tyres during the course of a Grand Prix weekend.**

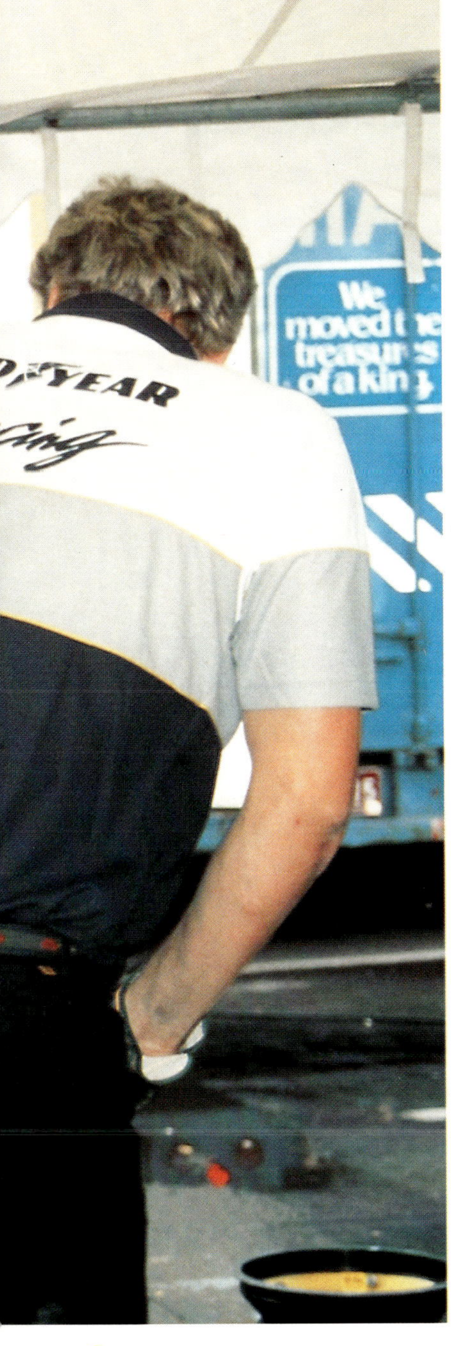

Engineering functions at the track include obtaining tyre temperatures to monitor the performance of the tyres, and to help the teams achieve optimum chassis set-up for the prevailing conditions. Mechanical changes in castor, camber and toe-in as well as the overall amount of understeer or oversteer displayed by a car are reflected in tyre temperature readings.

Tyre pressures are closely monitored and adjusted to achieve optimum balance between grip and stability. Tread wear measurements are taken to help plan the team's pit stop strategy, while wear patterns are also examined because they provide crucial additional clues to vehicle handling.

Finally, of course, driver input is absolutely essential. Comments from some of the world's most talented professional drivers play an indispensable role in determining the appropriate tyre selection decision and chassis suspension settings.

Back in the 1970s, there was no restriction on how many sets of qualifying tyres a competitor could use, but this was deemed too profligate and wasteful an arrangement. By 1981 a rule was introduced to limit each competitor to a couple of sets in each official qualifying session. Just to ensure that nobody is tempted to exceed the allotted maximum, FISA officials mark the chosen tyre sets prior to the start of qualifying. It is a system which Goodyear has always supported wholeheartedly.

'From a tyre company standpoint, this system put some sanity back into our racing programme,' explains Leo Mehl. 'We wouldn't want to return to the situation where it was permitted to throw unlimited sets of tyres at the cars. It didn't make a whole lot of sense.'

What Tony Shakespeare refers to as 'the lunchtime rush' can get particularly hectic if the teams are not sure what they are going to do, and take a long time reaching a conclusion as to which compounds they want, or if the occasional freak set of circumstances arise, as they did in practice for the 1990 Hungarian Grand Prix.

'That was absolutely horrendous for us,' Tony recalls. 'We introduced an alternative construction front tyre on the Saturday morning and let some people try it during the untimed session. We could have found ourselves facing a real emergency if everybody had wanted them for qualifying, because we'd have been in a position where 20-odd cars

Checking tread temperatures on Satoru Nakajima's 1989 Lotus 101-Judd.

needed to be kitted out with two different sets of front tyres each. Fortunately, not everybody opted to use them, so we were saved from facing a daunting workload which would have seen us sailing pretty close to the wind as far as the available time was concerned!'

Throughout the weekend a total of five engineers, in addition to Lee Gaug, Manager International Racing, will be carefully monitoring the performance of the Goodyear tyres in the pit lane. Almost every time a car stops, one of them will be there, checking the temperature spread across the surface of the tyre tread and monitoring the wear rate in detail. This information, combined with crucial input from the drivers involved, is fundamental to the task of gathering data on which to base future tyre development. By the end of the weekend, sufficient information will have been gathered for the engineers to make firm decisions on whether or not planned tyre specifications for future races need to be modified.

On the Sunday morning, the format follows much the same pattern with teams using the half-hour warm-up session to decide which of the available Goodyear race compounds they will choose for the serious business of the weekend. Once this has been determined, and even before the race has started, the Goodyear fitters are already preparing for the end of the day. Any tyres that are not wanted by the teams are returned to the tyre compound, removed from the rims and stowed away in the transporters.

Monitoring tread temperatures ***(opposite)*** **is one crucial aspect of the business of setting up a Grand Prix chassis to optimum levels of efficiency.**

The introduction of purpose-built semi-automatic tyre mounting machines is typical of Goodyear's thorough approach.

Once the race is over, they are faced with the task of dismounting another 400 or so tyres, a job for which the racing division has developed its own purpose-built machinery. Up until about 1986, the fitters had to work with manual tyre mounting tables but, thanks largely to Tony Shakespeare's suggestions, semi-automatic machines are now employed.

In a single operation, the wheel goes onto the table where it is clamped down hydraulically. While the fitter breaks the upper bead manually, four blades simultaneously break the lower bead. 'These were absolutely tailor-made for their purpose,' Tony explains. 'We told the company exactly what we wanted from the viewpoint of specification and they had them manufactured for us.'

Customs regulations demand that the Goodyear convoy return to England with precisely the same number of tyres it departed with and the company uses 'carnets' for the purposes of monitoring and recording the movements of tyres around the world. By about 21.00 on Sunday evening the transporters are generally fully loaded with discarded racing tyres and the whole cavalcade is ready to set off on its return journey. Generally the trucks get on the road on Monday morning, returning to Bushbury by Wednesday, which, at the height of the European racing season, effectively gives three or four days to ready the operation for departure to the next race.

Periodically, of course, there is a major disruption to the well-practised business of Goodyear's Formula 1 tyre supply programme. One such heart-stopping episode unfolded during the 1987 San Marino Grand Prix at Imola, an event which took place over the weekend of 1-3 May at a time when Akron's production facilities were stretched taut owing to the additional pressure of the Indianapolis 500 schedule.

This was at a time when the commercial demands of the moment had forced Goodyear into supplying only a control tyre to the F1 fraternity in an effort to retain some sort of a presence on the Grand Prix front. They arrived at Imola with a control tyre of a slightly different specification from that which had been used during the official pre-race test at the circuit a week or so before the GP.

The first signs of potential problems manifested themselves midway through the Friday morning untimed session when Goodyear engineers in the pit lane noticed that several rear covers were beginning to show the first signs of blistering along the crucial inner shoulder of the tread, a point always regarded as particularly critical as far as heat build-up is concerned.

Resourceful under pressure: Tony Shakespeare, Goodyear's Operations Manager.

Goodyear's technicians were all keeping a close eye on things when, midway through the first hour-long qualifying session, Nelson Piquet's Williams FW11B-Honda became involved in a very high speed accident. Nelson had been running hard, on his seventh successive lap, and had just posted the fastest time of the day, when his car spun wildly on the exit of the very fast Tamburello double-apex left-hander immediately after the pits.

The wayward machine slammed into the retaining wall on the outside of the circuit, fortunately careering in backwards to the point of impact, before ricocheting to a halt on the edge of the track. Although the situation looked quite serious for an agonising few seconds, Nelson did not suffer any long-term harm. After being taken to hospital in Bologna for a precautionary brain scan, he was back at the circuit the following morning, anxious that he should be permitted to continue competing. Prudently, FISA Medical Delegate Professor Syd Watkins decreed that he should not take part, so the Brazilian had to sit out this race on the sidelines.

However, pinning down the precise cause of the accident proved to be

Lee Gaug has been a familiar face in the F1 Goodyear camp since 1979.

When unforeseen problems arise, quick thinking is essential. Lee Gaug *(left)* **confers with Leo Mehl.**

an extremely difficult task. By the end of Friday afternoon, Williams Chief Designer Patrick Head had ruled out both driver error and component failure. 'The FW11B uses essentially the same suspension design that we have used ever since the Williams FW10 was designed at the end of 1984,' he asserted. 'It has proved totally reliable over two seasons of racing and there is no evidence to suggest it failed.'

This conclusion left the inevitable suspicion that tyre failure could have been the cause of the accident, particularly taking into account the erratic skid marks left on the track surface by the Williams-Honda's left-rear corner, just at the point where it would have been starting to load up again towards the end of the long left-hander. With this element of doubt hanging over the sequence of events, Goodyear promptly took the clear-sighted decision to withdraw all further supplies of this particular specification tyre. The result was a nerve-racking organisational headache.

'What followed was the closest call in my experience on the F1 scene,' recalls Lee Gaug. 'We never gave any thought to the possibility of withdrawing from the race, but we did have to think long and hard about what we were going to do. It took about two hours to sort out a plan of action.'

Tony Shakespeare takes up the story: 'We had to get onto the phone to Bushbury in order to find out what alternatives were available to us; you couldn't make the decision without knowing whether or not it was possible to replace them. Fortunately, we'd got some tyres in the same compound, albeit the previous construction, left over from Brazil where we had conserved more than expected. Once we had established that there were sufficient stocks in place, the next challenge was precisely how we were to get them to Imola.'

Goodyear's freight handling agent in England managed to locate a BAC 1-11 freighter which was available for charter, but it was based at Manston airport in Kent. Thus the 400 replacement tyres had to be transported halfway across England before the air journey could begin, a problem aggravated by the fact that all the racing division trucks were already away in Europe. Eventually a truck was borrowed from Goodyear's traffic department, arrangements were made with the customs authorities to speed up the necessary formalities at either end of the

GOODYEAR

Tyres discarded after the event must all be collected up and repacked in the Goodyear transporter. International 'carnet' regulations require that the same number of tyres are returned to the UK base as were originally exported.

trip and the tyres were duly delivered to Manston early on the Friday evening.

'All the arrangements were made, so it was now just a question of whether everything would fall in place,' recalls Tony Shakespeare. 'Just after midnight I got word that it had departed, so we got a vehicle ready and set off to Bologna airport. But it was then explained that the plane had only been able to take 350 of the 400 intended tyres. That left us agonising as to whether we were going to receive 250 front tyres and only 100 rears, rather than the 50-50 split we required. Mercifully one of our chaps from Bushbury had the foresight to realise that there had to be equal numbers of both tyres, so everything was OK, but we didn't know that until we arrived at Bologna airport and started unloading.

'When we arrived there the place seemed absolutely deserted, but seconds after the plane arrived at four o'clock in the morning all the necessary officials seemed to pop up out of the ground. Our vehicle was allowed out onto the tarmac, the tyres were off-loaded and we were back at Imola by six o'clock. We immediately began fitting up and were ready at nine o'clock. It was a close-run thing, but we decided on a fail-safe course in what was really an unexplained situation. We didn't want to risk anything.'

Of course, it is not simply technical pressures at the races which can throw a spanner into Goodyear's well-oiled works. After the San Marino Grand Prix in 1988, threats of a national dock and ferry strike in England left Goodyear's racing division in a state of uncertainty as to its transport strategy during the week following the race. If the transporter returned to Bushbury, there was a risk that it would be unable to reach Monaco for the Grand Prix a fortnight later.

Tony Shakespeare again: 'We didn't quite know what was going to happen. The dockers at Portsmouth were coming out and there were rumours that Dover would follow. The transporter was heading north through France, about three hours away from the ferry, when we decided to reroute it back to Nice.

'If we hadn't done that, we might have been in real trouble with no tyres available to Monaco unless we air-freighted in the entire allocation. In the end we chartered a huge Bristol Belfast freighter out of Stansted, shipped all the Monaco tyres down to Nice and sent it back with the

used covers that were left over from Imola. An operation like that is obviously very costly, but it's something out of the ordinary which proves immensely satisfying when it all works out correctly!'

For transport outside Europe, Goodyear relies on the Formula One Constructors' Association charters for material needing to be transported from Bushbury, but things can still go wrong on other fronts. For example, the 1990 Brazilian Grand Prix at Interlagos almost faced cancellation when the entire supply of tyres, which had been shipped by sea from the USA, was impounded by customs at Santos, the port of entry into Brazil near São Paulo.

At the time, Brazil was in the throes of a major economic crisis and Goodyear's local shipping agent was unable to find sufficient local currency to pay the duty on the tyres. The customs officials refused point-blank to release them and it was only when the Governor of São Paulo province intervened that the stalemate was broken late on the Wednesday evening prior to the race. The tyres were then released and rushed across to Interlagos just in time for Goodyear's contracted teams to take part in the unofficial practice session on the revised track the following day.

Most weekends, of course, the whole tyre supply system works to perfection with only the occasional minor setback. But the Goodyear racing division knows from personal experience just how suddenly and unexpectedly things can turn against it. Designing and manufacturing the tyres is truly only part of a much wider story.

GOODYEAR

250

GRAND PRIX WINS

Historic

3

Milestones

Honda made a preliminary foray onto the Grand Prix scene in 1964 when inexperienced American sports car driver Ronnie Bucknum gave the transverse-engined, V12-cylinder 1.5-litre prototype its maiden outing in the German Grand Prix at the Nürburgring. This exploratory dabble in the sport's most exalted category ended with Bucknum spinning off the road into retirement, after which the Japanese team returned home to ponder the magnitude of F1's challenge in preparation for a full-blown assault the following year.

Honda did not contest the first race of the '65 season, the South African Grand Prix at East London, on 1 January, preferring to hold back the debut of its two-car team for another five months, to the second round at Monaco on 30 May. However, Dan Gurney's Brabham BT11 turned out to practise for the South African race wearing Goodyear rubber for the first time.

Dan: 'I knew that Goodyear was not quite ready for top-line F1 competition, but I also realised that they intended to have a real go. So I decided to take the plunge and pull Jack [Brabham] in as well.' This deal reputedly added somewhere in the region of £10,000 to the Brabham F1 team's budget for the final year of the 1.5-litre formula; small beer by today's standards, but a very significant contribution at the time.

Neither Brabham had a trouble-free run in South Africa, but both Jack and Dan put on a remarkable display of Goodyear's potential in the non-title Race of Champions at Brands Hatch on 13 March. Gurney could only qualify on the fifth row of the grid after his car's Climax engine developed injection pump trouble during practice, but in the first 40-lap heat he was an absolute sensation as he carved through the pack to finish second behind Jim Clark's Lotus 33.

In the second heat Dan harried Clark with such remorseless ferocity that the Scot made a rare error of judgement under pressure and crashed heavily on Bottom Straight, thankfully emerging unhurt. The prospects for the Brabham/Goodyear alliance for the remainder of the season appeared extremely encouraging, but there were other mechanical problems which conspired to beset Gurney time and again when it looked as though he might genuinely get on terms with Clark's pace-setting Lotus in the World Championship battle.

At Monaco, the two-car Honda team, now on Goodyears, made its

Dan Gurney's Goodyear-shod Brabham-Climax heads for third place in the 1965 German Grand Prix at the Nürburgring.

debut with former BRM driver Richie Ginther now leading the Japanese squad and Bucknum as number two driver. They were both very badly off the pace, but as seeded runners claimed the last two positions on the grid. Ginther's car broke a driveshaft on the first lap, while Bucknum soldiered on until lap 33 when gear linkage problems ended his struggle.

With Dan Gurney and Jim Clark both away contesting the Indianapolis 500, the race was won for the third successive year by Graham Hill's BRM, although Brabham's Goodyear-shod machine again performed superbly, holding the lead from laps 34 to 42 when his 32-valve Climax V8 expired expensively. There were only two such extra-powerful Climax V8s in service during the '65 season, one earmarked for Clark's Lotus, the other for the Brabham team, where Gurney was generally assigned its priority use. Sadly for Dan, while the Lotus unit invariably performed with impressive reliability, his own efforts were constantly thwarted by mechanical breakages.

Goodyear's first World Championship points were scored at Spa-Francorchamps in the rain-soaked Belgian Grand Prix: Brabham finished fourth and Ginther brought the Honda home sixth. Clark won commandingly from Jackie Stewart's BRM. Only 12 months earlier, Gurney had been in a class of his own with the Brabham-Climax, dominating the race magnificently before running out of petrol on the final lap. This year, however, there was to be no repeat performance in the torrential conditions and Dan trailed round to finish a disappointed tenth, unhappy with his car's precarious handling.

During the balance of the season, Dan's best placings would be third in the German Grand Prix at the Nürburgring and a storming second at Mexico City in the final round of the championship. This was the event, of course, in which Ginther produced an outstanding showing to win for Honda and Goodyear.

After just nine attempts, Honda scored its first Grand Prix triumph, Ginther running with the leaders right from the start of practice at the Autodromo Magdalena Mixhuca. Prior to this event, Honda had spent two days of private testing at the circuit and adjusted the fuel injection system to its optimum in order to cater for the altitude, some 7000 ft above sea level.

GOODYEAR WINS!

Mexican Grand Prix

1st Richie Ginther
HONDA

2nd Dan Gurney
BRABHAM/CLIMAX

This is the tyre that won for Richie Ginther driving a Honda

It's built with Goodyear's exclusive 3-T cord pound-for-pound stronger than steel – and tough Tufsyn rubber, to withstand the tyre's scorching pace and punishment of the world's fastest racing circuits.

This is the tyre for your car.
It's the G-8 by Goodyear – built with the same exclusive 3-T cord construction and tough Tufsyn rubber. The same development and research which goes into Goodyear's top performance tyres goes into the G-8 for your family car.

Subject to official confirmation

GOODYEAR

In the event, Clark's Lotus 33 took pole position on 1m 56.17s with Gurney next in the Brabham (1m 56.24s) and Ginther on the inside of the second row. Even Bucknum demonstrated the benefit of that extra day's testing by returning a 1m 57.88s, which was enough to put him tenth on the 17-car grid.

Race day proved even hotter than the two practice days, and when it came to the start there was no matching the combination of Ginther, Honda and Goodyear. The freckle-faced Californian grabbed the lead going into the first corner and never looked back.

'I glanced in my mirror at the end of the first lap,' he later recounted, 'and just didn't see a soul until I was clear past the end of the pits. I thought I must have dropped a gallon of oil and that they had all spun off behind me!'

Ginther quickly built up a seven-second lead over Mike Spence's works Lotus before the Englishman succumbed to a strong challenge from Gurney's Brabham after 18 laps. For the rest of the race Dan threw everything he had into a strong counter-attack, but the Honda V12 was certainly superior to the Climax V8 on this occasion and Ginther wasn't making any errors.

Richie seemed to have plenty in reserve, gauging his progress by noting Gurney's relative position as he accelerated out of the hairpin on each lap. He rationed himself to 11,000 rpm throughout the race, but if Gurney looked as though he was making up too much ground Ginther would use 11,500 of the Honda's available 12,000 rpm just to settle the issue. He eventually notched up Goodyear's first Grand Prix victory – a 1-2, of course, for Dan was also on Goodyears – by the scant margin of 2.8 seconds.

Early success celebrated: this advertisement recording Ginther's 1965 Mexico win appeared in the prestigious American magazine *Road and Track*.

Richie Ginther's delight is written all over his face as he is fêted after his victory in the 1965 Mexican Grand Prix.

GOODYEAR

Jack Brabham heads his Brabham BT19-Repco towards victory in the 1966 Dutch Grand Prix at Zandvoort, one of four wins which helped him to his third championship title – and Goodyear's first.

1966 Jack Brabham Brabham – Repco

Dan Gurney joined the Brabham team as a Goodyear runner when he launched his AAR Eagle in 1966.

Dan Gurney had, by now, become very anxious to achieve sustained success and, after lengthy talks with Goodyear and Esso – Brabham's fuel sponsor – opted to go his own way and branch out with his own All American Racers Eagle project for the new 3-litre F1 which came into force at the start of 1966.

The new Eagles would also be fitted with Goodyear tyres, in addition to the Brabham and Honda teams, and 1966 would see Goodyear win its maiden World Championship thanks to the efforts of Jack Brabham's Repco-engined machine which started the year very much as an outside threat.

At the time, much was made of the potential of the new Ferrari 312 and Cooper T81-Maserati, both of which initially ran on Dunlops before Maranello's mid-season switch to Firestones. Brabham, however, persuaded the Melbourne-based Repco organisation to develop a 3-litre version of the light alloy Oldsmobile V8 which had originally been adapated, in 2.5-litre guise, for the Tasman formula, Australia's most prestigious single-seater category.

Installed in a light, agile spaceframe chassis, it displayed just the right blend of performance and reliability to be a consistent threat over the season as a whole. An indication of possible future form came in one of the traditional pre-season warm-ups, the non-title BRDC International Trophy race at Silverstone. Brabham won easily, beating Surtees's much-touted Ferrari in a straight fight, and although Jack was then out of luck at Monaco and Spa he became the first driver in a car bearing his own name to win a World Championship Grand Prix in the French race at Reims.

This was followed up by a succession of victories in the British Grand Prix at Brands Hatch, the Dutch Grand Prix at Zandvoort and the German Grand Prix at the Nürburgring, by which time the championship was as good as settled.

1967 Denny Hulme Brabham – Repco

Denny Hulme on his way to victory at Monaco in 1967 with the Brabham BT20-Repco. He would win again at the Nürburgring later in the year and go on to earn another World Championship for Brabham and Goodyear.

Share the secret behind two world championships...

Goodyear Tyremanship!

Denny Hulme had Goodyear Tyremanship right behind him all the way to the 1967 World Grand Prix Championship. So did last year's winner, Jack Brabham. But WHAT IS Goodyear Tyremanship?

Goodyear Tyremanship isn't something you can weigh or measure. Nor can you *buy* it. It's Goodyear's.

But you can *share* it.

Goodyear Tyremanship is a unique recipe of experience, know-how, resources, size, skill, efficiency—and above all, sheer will-to-win. It's the quality with which Goodyear has dominated the world racing scene the last few years—the quality that puts top features into every Goodyear tyre *you* buy.

Check them. Tufsyn rubber. 3T cord. Wraparound tread. They're Goodyear exclusives. Whether you choose crossply tyres or radials, choose Goodyear.

Get Goodyear Tyremanship on YOUR side.

Goodyear 1967 wins include Indianapolis 500, Shell 4000 Rally, Race of Champions at Brands Hatch, Monaco Grand Prix, Le Mans 24-Hour Race, Belgian Grand Prix, French Grand Prix, German Grand Prix, Canadian Grand Prix.

The Brabham contract produced a second World Championship in 1967, this time with Jack's number two Denny Hulme squeezing out all the Brabham BT24-Repco had to give. The massive, square-shouldered Goodyears, designed at Bushbury by the British design team led by Walt deVinney, provided the vital rubber on the road for these successes. Honda, meanwhile, after a barren 1966 season, switched to Firestone, but Bruce McLaren's fledgling Grand Prix team had effectively taken its place in the Goodyear fold.

Formula 1 obviously consolidated its role as Goodyear's most prestigious category, although during 1966 Goodyear tyres had also carried rally cars to victory in the Acropolis, RAC and Canadian Shell 4000 events and Ford GT40s to wins at Daytona, Sebring and Le Mans. In 1967 Gurney and A.J. Foyt would score Goodyear's third straight Le Mans win and McLaren crushed all opposition to take the Can-Am Championship title.

Technical development continued apace during these early years. Goodyear's race tyre treads had grown from 5 to 6 inches in width during 1965, thence to 7½ inches in 1966 and up to a massive 10 inches in 1967. In time for the 1968 South African Grand Prix at Kyalami they were up to 11½ inches and an improved cross-ply construction was introduced at the same time, continuing the distinctively low-profile outline which had become one of the Goodyear hallmarks at the time.

A new compound – known as G4 – was introduced in time for Bruce

McLaren to give the new McLaren M7-Cosworth a fine debut win in the '68 Brands Hatch Race of Champions, with Denny Hulme scoring a follow-up success at the Silverstone International Trophy. However, that was almost as far as it went in 1968 as Graham Hill's Lotus 49B won the World Championship on Firestones by a close margin from Jackie Stewart's Dunlop-shod Matra MS10.

In 1969 Stewart had the upper hand, dominating the season to win the first of three World Championships and, although nobody could know

Bruce McLaren's new McLaren M7-Cosworth scored a commanding debut victory in the 1968 Race of Champions at Brands Hatch, laying the foundations of the F1 team which dominates Grand Prix racing to this day.

Jacky Ickx took his Goodyear-shod Brabham to a famous victory in the German Grand Prix in 1969, conquering World Champion Jackie Stewart in the process.

it at the time, the only one not achieved on Goodyear rubber. The tempo of tyre development was hotting up to the point where it was becoming necessary to tailor individual compounds to specific circuits. Consequently, it was with some satisfaction that Goodyear perfected its new G18 compound in time for the German Grand Prix at the Nürburgring, where Jacky Ickx's Brabham eased out Stewart's Matra to score a worthy triumph. That put Goodyear back in play, and a further-developed G20 compound helped Ickx to win again in Canada and Denny Hulme's McLaren to triumph in Mexico.

The following year Jackie was to have a difficult time wrestling with

Top: **Denny Hulme and Bruce McLaren: loyal Goodyear supporters in both F1 and Can-Am between 1968 and '70.**

Centre: **Jack Brabham, Ron Tauranac, Jacky Ickx and Leo Mehl look pleased with their efforts after the Belgian's victory in the 1969 Canadian Grand Prix.**

Princess Margaret on a visit to Bushbury during the summer of '68.

1971 Jackie Stewart Tyrrell – Ford

Jack Brabham's Brabham BT33 won the 1970 South African Grand Prix at Kyalami, the last F1 success of the Australian's distinguished career.

Journalists Bernard Cahier *(left)* and Jabby Crombac *(right)* share a joke with Jack Brabham and Leo Mehl.

the Dunlop-shod March 701, being forced to sit back and watch Firestone users Lotus romp the title chase with the trend-setting 72, and this frustration helped steer Stewart and the Tyrrell team into the Goodyear camp for 1971, thereby creating one of the most spectacularly productive racing partnerships in recent F1 history.

Jackie and Ken shrewdly appreciated that the key to unlocking the door of sustained Grand Prix success lay in an intensive programme of test and development work. It is probably fair to say that, together, Stewart, Tyrrell and Goodyear in effect wrote the definitive F1 tyre testing handbook, setting a trend which is sustained to this day.

From the very start of 1971, Jackie committed himself to intensive test sessions at tracks all over the world, and this commitment enabled Goodyear to become the first F1 tyre supplier to find a technical solution to the punishing vibration problems which were afflicting all F1 cars at the time. 'The vibrations were so severe that you could hear the machine-gun-like chatter a mile off,' recalls Leo Mehl.

Goodyear was also the first to introduce slick-treaded tyres, in time for the inaugural French GP at Paul Ricard, and was by now forcing a dramatic pace on the Grand Prix scene. Dunlop had dropped out at the end of the 1970 season, leaving Firestone to battle against its Akron rivals through to the end of 1974.

After Stewart had dominated the '71 championship chase with victories in the Spanish, Monaco, French, British and German Grands Prix, Firestone counter-attacked the following season to help Emerson Fittipaldi and Lotus snatch the title.

Leo Mehl had returned to Akron at the end of 1971, his position as

Jackie Stewart led the 1971 French Grand Prix at Paul Ricard from start to finish in his Tyrrell on Goodyear's newly introduced slick tyres.

BP
elf

GOODYEAR
elf
STEWART
GOODYEAR
4
elf
4
Ford

Twelve months later, Jackie *(left)* repeated his success in the French race, this time staged at Clermont-Ferrand.

Racing manager Ed Alexander in company with engineer Bert Baldwin.

Goodyear's European Director of Racing being taken by Ed Alexander, who presided over the development of prototype 14-inch wide tyres to replace the year-old 13-inch size after the '72 Belgian Grand Prix at Nivelles. Initial testing seemed extremely promising and, with contracted teams securing supplies of the appropriately sized wheel rims, these new rears were taken to Clermont-Ferrand for the French Grand Prix, which Stewart would win with the new Goodyears finishing first, third, fourth, fifth and seventh.

Concurrent experiments were also progressing with a dragster-like tyre construction, nicknamed the 'wrinkle wall', which was designed to wind up under power like a huge spring literally to catapult a car away from slow corners. This slingshot quality produced considerable benefit, and worked to particularly good effect, on tight circuits rather than on the faster tracks where the established low-profile tyre offered more secure handling thanks to the stability conferred by its shallower sidewalls.

This programme paid off during the summer of '72, and at Mosport Park Ronnie Peterson used these tyres to qualify his March 721G second on the grid for the Canadian Grand Prix, challenging for the lead in the early stages before he encountered mechanical problems. Jackie Stewart eventually won the race for Tyrrell and Goodyear, going on to round off the season with an impressive victory run in the US Grand Prix at Watkins Glen, achievements which provided major PR consolation for Firestone's overall championship success.

During the winter of 1972-73, Firestone's uncertainty over future F1

The final Grand Prix win of Stewart's career was achieved in the '73 German race at the Nürburgring where he is seen leading team-mate François Cevert, who finished a strong second.

Schallplatten
GOODYEAR
elf
elf
5

Jacky Ickx ***(below)*** **scored the only victory of his Lotus career at the wheel of the Lotus 72 in the rain-drenched 1974 Brands Hatch Race of Champions.**

plans enabled Goodyear to score a major coup by bringing Team Lotus into its fold, so although the '73 drivers' and constructors' titles went to separate destinations (Jackie Stewart and Lotus respectively) it still amounted to a Goodyear double. Throughout the 1972 and '73 seasons, Firestone could take comfort in the performance of its wet-weather rubber, exemplified by the splendid victory of Jean-Pierre Beltoise for BRM at Monaco in '72, but Goodyear did not take long to strengthen this element in its armoury: in the rain-soaked '74 Race of Champions at Brands Hatch, the quickest Goodyear runner lapped its fastest Firestone rival in a scant ten laps!

At the end of 1974, Firestone quit the Grand Prix scene, leaving Goodyear with a monopoly situation. This not only presented Bushbury with the challenge of expanding its output to service a tyre supply monopoly over the years 1975–77, but also posed the complex question of how to handle the business of long-term technical development in a situation where, temporarily at least, it had no opposition against which to measure its on-track efforts.

By now Ed Alexander's stint as Director of Racing was over and his

1973 Jackie Stewart Tyrrell – Ford

Ronnie Peterson and Emerson Fittipaldi running in tight formation on their way to a Lotus 1-2 in the 1973 Italian Grand Prix at Monza. Although Stewart won that year's drivers' title, Lotus took the constructors' championship, also running on Goodyears.

1974 Emerson Fittipaldi McLaren – Ford

Checking tyre pressures on James Hunt's McLaren M23 prior to the 1976 British Grand Prix at Brands Hatch.

Niki Lauda's first World Championship was achieved with Ferrari in 1975. Driving for the Italian team, the Austrian quickly forged a reputation as a shrewd race tactician as well as a sensitive and perceptive tyre tester.

1975 Niki Lauda Ferrari

CYCLONE
LUCKY STRIKE
GOOD YEAR
Niki Lauda
GOOD YEAR
Agip
HEUER
1
GOOD YEAR
Agip

James Hunt's superb driving in the rain during the 1976 Japanese Grand Prix at Mount Fuji earned him the World Championship by a single point from Lauda, the Englishman scrambling back to finish third after a late-race stop to replace a deflated front tyre.

place was taken by Denny Chrobak, under whose auspices the company began to explore an ambitious Vehicles Dynamic Programme in which a number of F1 cars were kitted out with complex measuring instruments in an attempt accurately to research their behaviour at racing speeds. This programme was under the control of Dr Karl Kempf, a physics Ph.D., and lasted through to the start of 1978 when Kempf left to continue a similar project full-time on behalf of the Tyrrell team. Alexander returned to the US where he sadly died a few years later from a brain tumour.

Ferrari proved particularly willing to collaborate on this VDP programme, although its enthusiasm would turn out to be something of a double-edged sword as the Italian team became slightly disgruntled when tyres it had done most of the development testing on proved even more competitive when fitted to rival manufacturers' chassis!

When Goodyear's offerings seemed particularly suited to James Hunt's McLaren M23 during the 1976 season, performing even better than they did on the Ferrari 312T2 driven by Niki Lauda, Enzo Ferrari himself launched some blistering attacks upon his tyre supplier and all Ferrari road cars destined for stands at international motor shows rather unsubtly appeared wearing Michelin radial rubber. It was an episode which certainly underlined how difficult it is to satisfy all the people all the time in the Grand Prix tyre supply business.

As a fascinating technical aside, in 1976 Goodyear also produced some tiny 10-inch diameter front tyres – the smallest ever manufactured for an F1 application – to fit the radical Tyrrell P34 six-wheeler. This dramatic

In the pit lane at Kyalami, Lauda waits patiently while engineers work on his Ferrari 312T during practice for the 1976 South African Grand Prix. He won this race commandingly from James Hunt's McLaren.

1976 James Hunt McLaren – Ford

In 1976 Goodyear manufactured special 10-inch diameter front tyres for the Tyrrell P34 six-wheeler, seen *(overleaf)* ***en route*** **to its sole victory in the hands of Jody Scheckter in Sweden.**

GOODYEAR
SCHECKTER
CHAMPION
KONI

3
elf
elf

Goodyear makes effective promotional use of its products' wet-weather qualities; this 1977 advertisement features a rain-soaked Ronnie Peterson in the Tyrrell P34 six-wheeler.

experiment on the part of Tyrrell designer Derek Gardner was initiated in an attempt to increase front-end grip while at the same time reducing the car's frontal area. Although Jody Scheckter and Patrick Depailler would finish first and second in that year's Swedish Grand Prix at Anderstorp, and Tyrrell persevered with the project through to the end of 1977, it was not a concept imitated by others and had no long-term future.

Into the 1977 season Goodyear became increasingly mindful of the planned Renault turbo F1 challenge which was scheduled to bring rival Michelin radial technology to the forefront of Grand Prix competition. In addition to continuing instrumented VDP tests across a wide range of teams, both the Wolf and Brabham teams were recruited to run instrumented tests at Goodyear's international test centre in Luxembourg in order to amass as much knowledge as possible for a head-to-head battle with Michelin.

In fact, this battle did not seriously transpire until 1978 when Ferrari joined Renault in using Michelin's new radial tyres, by which time Goodyear had reached a significant personal landmark by scoring its 100th Grand Prix victory. This red-letter day came at Hockenheim in the summer of '77 when Niki Lauda, one year after almost losing his life in a fiery accident at the Nürburgring, won the German Grand Prix for Ferrari. To celebrate this accomplishment, Goodyear invited along Richie Ginther, the man who scored its first such triumph in Mexico, to witness the long-term fruits produced by his efforts 12 years earlier!

That same summer, fifty years of Goodyear tyre manufacture at Bushbury were celebrated by a visit from Her Majesty The Queen, who toured the entire plant, including the racing division.

Of course, the 1977 season had seen Colin Chapman pioneer ground-

Hockenheim, 1977. Ferrari's tyre supply with covers specifically marked for the use of Niki Lauda and Carlos Reutemann on the weekend of Goodyear's 100th victory.

18/10
SET. 1
HIKI
R
18/10
SET. 1
CARLOS
L
18/10
SET. 1
HIKI
L
18/10
SET. 1
CARLOS
R
23/18
SET. 1
HIKI
L
23/18
SET. 1
CARLOS
R
23/18
SET. 1
HIKI
R
23/18
SET. 1
CARLOS
L

1977 Niki Lauda Ferrari

Niki Lauda's 1977 victory in the German GP at Hockenheim was Goodyear's 100th Grand Prix win.

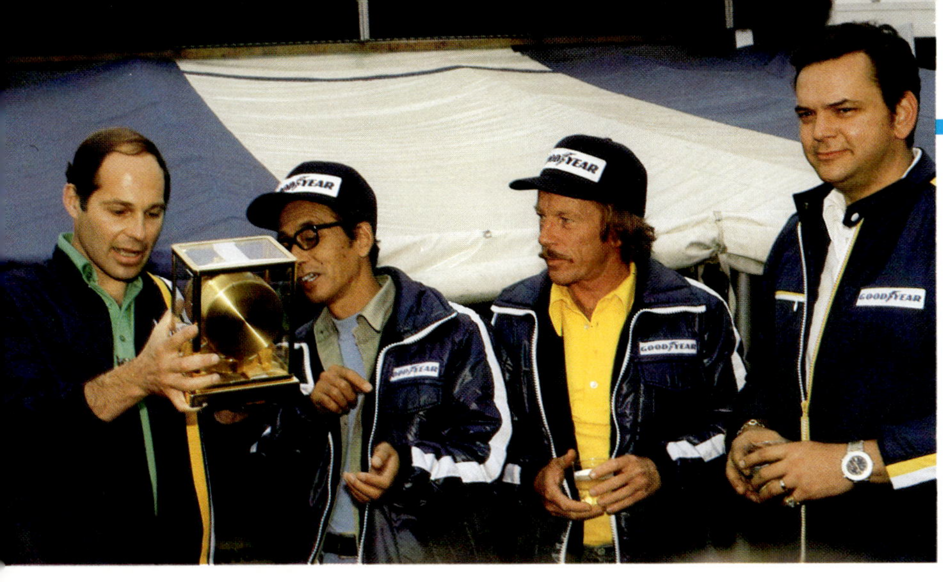

In anticipation of Goodyear's 100th win, Richie Ginther (second from right next to Denny Chrobak) was invited to Hockenheim some 12 years after his historic victory for Honda in Mexico.

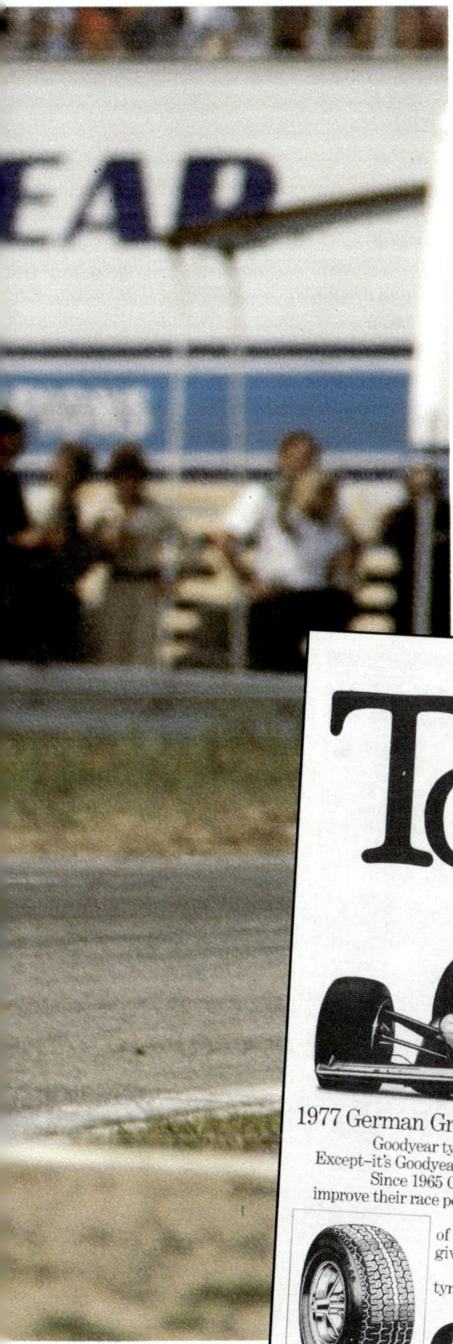

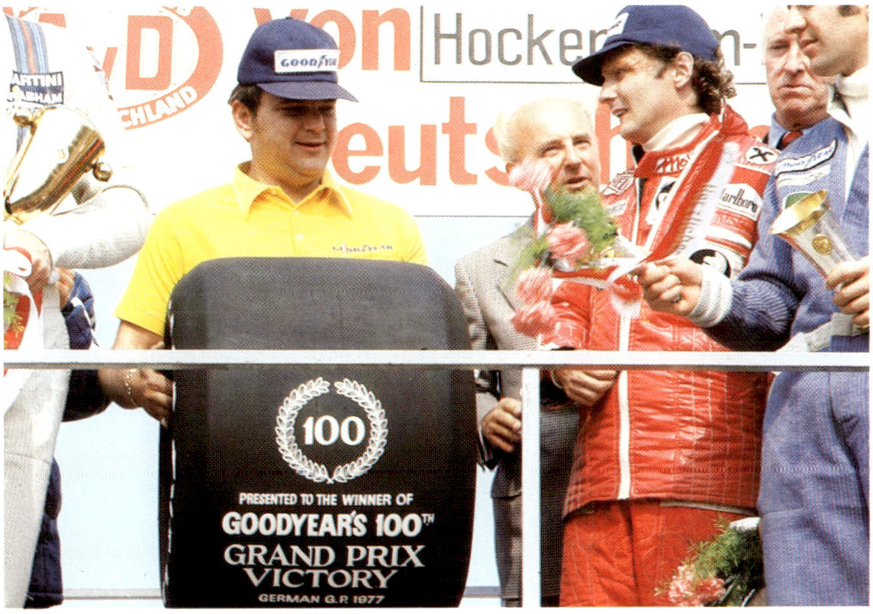
100
PRESENTED TO THE WINNER OF
GOODYEAR'S 100TH
GRAND PRIX
VICTORY
GERMAN G.P. 1977

Above: **Goodyear's Denny Chrobak prepares to make a presentation to Niki Lauda on the victory rostrum at Hockenheim, 1977.**

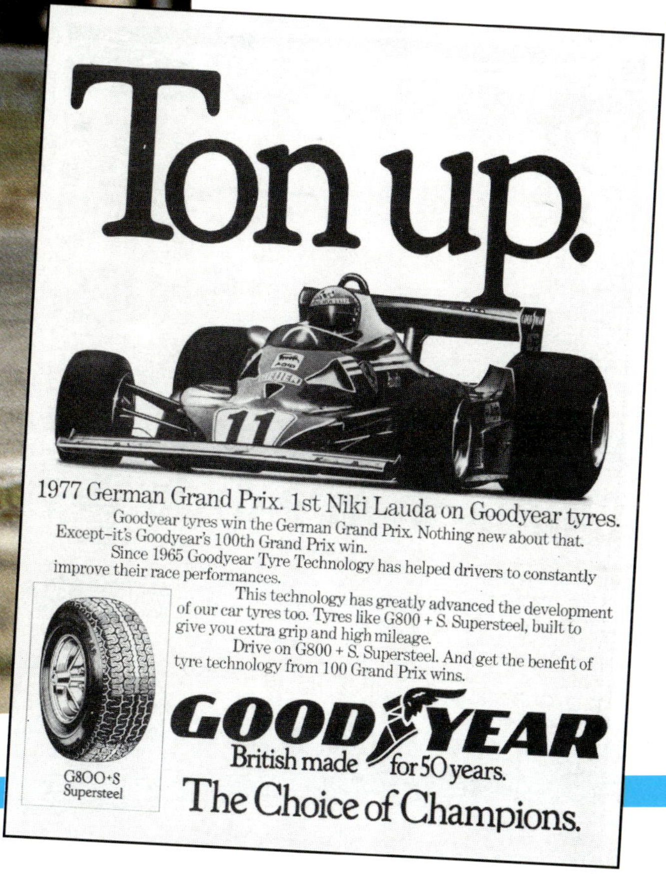
Ton up.
1977 German Grand Prix. 1st Niki Lauda on Goodyear tyres.
Goodyear tyres win the German Grand Prix. Nothing new about that. Except–it's Goodyear's 100th Grand Prix win.
Since 1965 Goodyear Tyre Technology has helped drivers to constantly improve their race performances.
This technology has greatly advanced the development of our car tyres too. Tyres like G800 + S. Supersteel, built to give you extra grip and high mileage.
Drive on G800 + S. Supersteel. And get the benefit of tyre technology from 100 Grand Prix wins.
G800+S Supersteel
GOODYEAR
British made for 50 years.
The Choice of Champions.

Blowing the Goodyear trumpets after the company's 100th Grand Prix win, Hockenheim, 1977.

Denny Chrobak was Goodyear's F1 racing manager in the field from 1976–78.

The jackets of the prestigious *Autocourse* annual, overprinted specially for Goodyear, celebrating the company's World Championship successes of 1977 (Niki Lauda/ Ferrari) and 1978 (Mario Andretti/ Lotus).

Jody Scheckter opened the 1977 season with a well-judged win for Wolf, Ford and Goodyear in the Argentine Grand Prix at Buenos Aires.

effect technology with the advent of the new Lotus 78, which harnessed under-car aerodynamics to dramatically competitive effect. But for an unfortunate spate of engine failures, Mario Andretti would have emerged as World Champion, but he would carry the Goodyear standard to the 1978 title, beating off a challenge from Carlos Reutemann's Ferrari, which won four races on Michelin radials.

The size of Goodyear's task in '78 could not be underestimated, for Michelin had only two Ferraris and a single Renault to service on an exclusive basis. Thus although Goodyear had such potentially front-running teams as Lotus, Brabham, Tyrrell, Williams and Wolf on its books it also assumed the obligation of servicing the balance of the field.

Throughout the season Akron produced a wide range of qualifying compounds, although it was not until the final race in Montreal that it managed to extend its supply to all 27 Goodyear runners. Competitive pressures being such as they were, it was only to be expected that the company should take a selective view when it came to supplying these qualifying tyres, and such a priority system was an inevitable by-product of the situation in which Goodyear found itself. Such a state of affairs called for considerable tact and diplomacy on the part of Goodyear's latest racing manager, Paul Lauritzen, who took over from Denny Chrobak at the start of the year. Denny remained with Goodyear in Akron where today he works on advanced tyre designs in the company's technical centre.

1978 Mario Andretti Lotus – Ford

AUTOCOURSE
1977-78
With the compliments of
GOODYEAR
THE CHOICE OF CHAMPIONS
AUTOCOURSE
1978-79
John Player Special
With the compliments of
GOODYEAR
THE CHOICE OF CHAMPIONS
heckter
Walter Wolf Racing
20

GOODYEAR
RACING TYRES
VALVOLINE
John Player Special
OLYMPUS
CAMERAS
GOOD YEAR
5
Valvoline
Valvoline

Opposite: **Another Goodyear championship team: Andretti and Peterson with the Lotus crew, the class of 1978.**

Mario and Ronnie in close company during the 1978 Dutch Grand Prix at Zandvoort, their final 1-2 finish of the season with the sensational ground-effect Lotus 79s.

Clay Regazzoni scored loyal Goodyear user Frank Williams's first Grand Prix win at Silverstone in 1979 with the epochal Patrick Head-designed Williams FW07.

Alan Jones receives a commemorative clock in celebration of his achievement in scoring Goodyear's 125th Grand Prix victory. *From left to right:* **Leo Mehl, Jones, Jackie Stewart and racing manager Paul Lauritzen.**

Michelin grabbed the World Championship with Ferrari in 1979, but while Lotus dropped from the high wire as Goodyear's most competitive runner its place was taken by the outstanding Williams FW07, in which Clay Regazzoni gave Frank's team a maiden Grand Prix victory at Silverstone. Thereafter Alan Jones began a late burst for the championship, adding four more wins at Hockenheim, the Österreichring, Zandvoort and Montreal to the Williams/Goodyear tally and finishing third in the title chase.

At the end of 1979, the manufacture of all racing tyres reverted to Akron and the race tyre manufacturing facility at Bushbury was closed, although the F1 service division remained there. Economic considerations were at the root of this decision – the UK tyre market was not in the best of health at the time – and a purpose-built new racing department had been established in Akron.

Leo Mehl: 'The shift of F1 tyre manufacturing from Bushbury to Akron was primarily to pursue the development of radial tyres for Grand Prix purposes. It became obvious that it was going to take a great corporate effort to develop the radial, so the international effort in Wolverhampton was consolidated with the US-based engineers such as Stu Grant and Perry Bell, who were also charged with converting all the American racing tyres to radial construction.

'The massive effort would also require considerable assistance from all the various technical arms at Goodyear, such as machine design and fabric development.

'In addition to developing the radial, the other primary reason for the move was the large technical centre facility available in Akron. This had been expanded to consolidate all the racing tyres under one roof. This further enhanced a great asset that Goodyear has sustained from the start of its racing involvement – namely the best manufacturing and producing group in the industry.

'We can claim to manufacture several hundred thousand racing tyres each year and maintain the build quality. Our highly skilled workforce has been our "secret weapon" ever since the racing tyre wars started in the 1960s. There are literally dozens of Goodyear employees who have made a significant contribution to the 250 Grand Prix victories achieved by the company.'

Thumbs-up from Alan Jones, 1980 World Champion on Goodyear rubber.

1980 Alan Jones Williams – Ford

For 1980, Michelin was forced to take a back seat through a combination of Ferrari uncompetitiveness and Renault mechanical unreliability, Goodyear sweeping to victory in all but three races, with Jones and Williams clinching the championship in commanding style. The year was also highlighted by Nelson Piquet's first Grand Prix victory at Long Beach, a portent of great things to come on the part of the Brazilian driver, who would go on to win two of his three World Championships (1981 and '87) and 14 of his 22 Grand Prix victories on Goodyear products.

On Bushbury's closure Paul Lauritzen returned to Akron, where he is now Sales Director for the Racing Tyre Division, and his place in the F1 pit lanes was taken by the pipe-smoking Lee Gaug, a former fighter pilot in the US Marine Corps who flew in the Korean war. Prior to becoming involved in F1, Lee had spent ten years working for Goodyear on sports car racing programmes in the USA.

By the end of 1980, Formula 1 had developed into an uncomfortably political business and the predominantly British teams aligned with the Formula One Constructors' Association (FOCA) seemed on the verge of a damaging split with the sport's governing body, FISA. The problem arose over FISA's decision to ban sliding aerodynamic side skirts, ostensibly in the interests of safety, but the FOCA lobby saw this move as a deliberate attempt to undermine the competitiveness of its member teams in favour of the FISA-aligned *Grande Costruttori* – Renault and Ferrari – both of whom were in the forefront of turbo engine development.

Things got so bad that there was even talk of a breakaway championship to be run under the aegis of the 'World Federation of Motor Sport' and, faced with this long-term uncertainty, Goodyear took the decision to bow off the Grand Prix stage in November 1980. Happily, matters were regularised by the following summer, when the company felt able to return, initially to service only Brabham and Williams, from the French Grand Prix onwards. During its absence, the boot had been very much on the other foot with Michelin suddenly finding itself obliged to provide tyres for the entire Grand Prix field through the first half of 1981.

'At that time, although we were committed to people in F1 and to the

Congratulations Alan Jones and the Saudia Williams Leyland team on a fantastic season on Goodyear.
GOODYEAR
AUTOSPORT, OCTOBER 2, 1980
7

The first victory of Nelson Piquet's distinguished Grand Prix career came at Long Beach in 1980 with this Brabham BT49-Cosworth.

development of the product, the political situation between FOCA and FISA had become so bad that we figured there was no way we could recover the investment we had in the business,' explained Leo Mehl. 'It is very difficult to equate the return on one's investment in motor racing, but with all that controversy going on we decided that we did not wish to be associated with it through that period.

'As you can imagine, participation in a racing programme the size of Goodyear's requires a significant budget. Any sizeable budget within a large corporation is, quite rightly, inevitably the subject for some debate. There are always those who say the money could be better spent elsewhere.

'After our withdrawal, there were a number of happy executives who had never believed in the racing programme. Now the extra money was available, but what to do with it? As it turned out, it was impossible to get an equal "bang for the buck" as we got from racing. Any doubts as to the value of the programme were quickly removed.

'The major shock, of course, came to the racing personnel when they found how far things had proceeded technically in our short absence. It basically took a maximum effort for two years to catch up with what we had missed being away from F1 for six months!'

Although Prost won three Grands Prix for Renault and Michelin, the '81 championship eventually came down to a battle between Brabham and Williams at the final race of the season at Las Vegas. Alan Jones won the race commandingly, clinching a second constructors' title for Frank, but Piquet just edged out Reutemann for the drivers' crown, the Brazilian staggering home a dehydrated and exhausted fifth, three places ahead of his Argentinian rival.

The Brabham team's mid-season switch from Michelin to Goodyear is capitalised on in this 1981 championship success advertisement featuring Nelson Piquet.

1981 Nelson Piquet Brabham – Ford

1966. Jack Brabham Formula 1 World Champion on Goodyear.
1967. Denis Hulme Formula 1 World Champion on Goodyear.
1971. Jackie Stewart Formula 1 World Champion on Goodyear.
1973. Jackie Stewart Formula 1 World Champion on Goodyear.
1974. Emerson Fittipaldi Formula 1 World Champion on Goodyear.
1975. Niki Lauda Formula 1 World Champion on Goodyear.
1976. James Hunt Formula 1 World Champion on Goodyear.
1977. Niki Lauda Formula 1 World Champion on Goodyear.
1978. Mario Andretti Formula 1 World Champion on Goodyear.
1980. Alan Jones Formula 1 World Champion on Goodyear.

1981. Nelson Piquet switched to Goodyear and won the World Championship.

Keke Rosberg at the wheel of the Williams FW08 prior to the 1982 Belgian Grand Prix at Zolder. The flying Finn scored only a single victory that season, but took Williams and Goodyear to the title in the face of a strong Michelin challenge from McLaren and Renault.

1982 Keke Rosberg Williams – Ford

In 1982 Goodyear again successfully staved off Michelin's challenge, providing the equipment on which Keke Rosberg vanquished the increasingly dominant turbos at the wheel of his Williams FW08-Cosworth. With Nelson Piquet's Brabham-BMW turbo winning the first forced-induction title in '83, Goodyear had to take second place to Michelin's endeavours, although Patrick Tambay's Ferrari 126C2B turbo scored a sweet win at Imola and Rosberg a dynamic triumph at Monte Carlo in the naturally aspirated Williams FW08C. Akron was still using cross-ply construction at this point, but the technical pressure

Overleaf: **René Arnoux leads Ferrari team-mate Patrick Tambay on the opening lap of the 1983 San Marino Grand Prix at Imola. Tambay scored a commanding win after Riccardo Patrese's Michelin-shod Brabham-BMW crashed in the closing stages.**

RENAULT
RENAULT
GOODYEAR
GOODYEAR
GOODYEAR
Agip
28

GIACOBAZZI
LAMBRUSCO
RENAULT
RENAULT
RENAULT
27
11

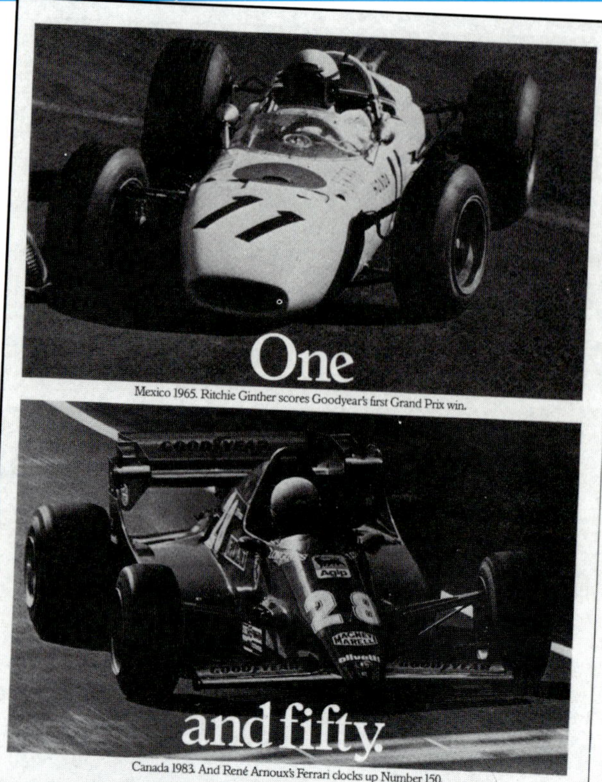

One
Mexico 1965. Ritchie Ginther scores Goodyear's first Grand Prix win.
and fifty.
Canada 1983. And René Arnoux's Ferrari clocks up Number 150.
hundred
Germany 1977. Niki Lauda's Ferrari makes it 100 victories for our tyres.
Since our first Grand Prix win back in 1965 twelve Formula 1 World Championships have been won on our tyres, ten in the last twelve years.
And that's included an amazing one hundred and fifty race victories.
Our unbeatable experience on the track is reflected in the development of our road tyres.
Tyres like the Goodyear NCT. A low profile, high performance tyre, it can bring out the best in your car.
Just like our tyres did for René in Montreal.
GOODYEAR
Choice of Champions.

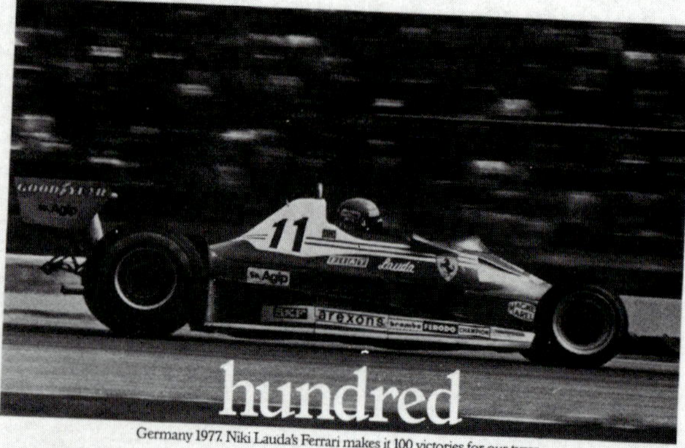

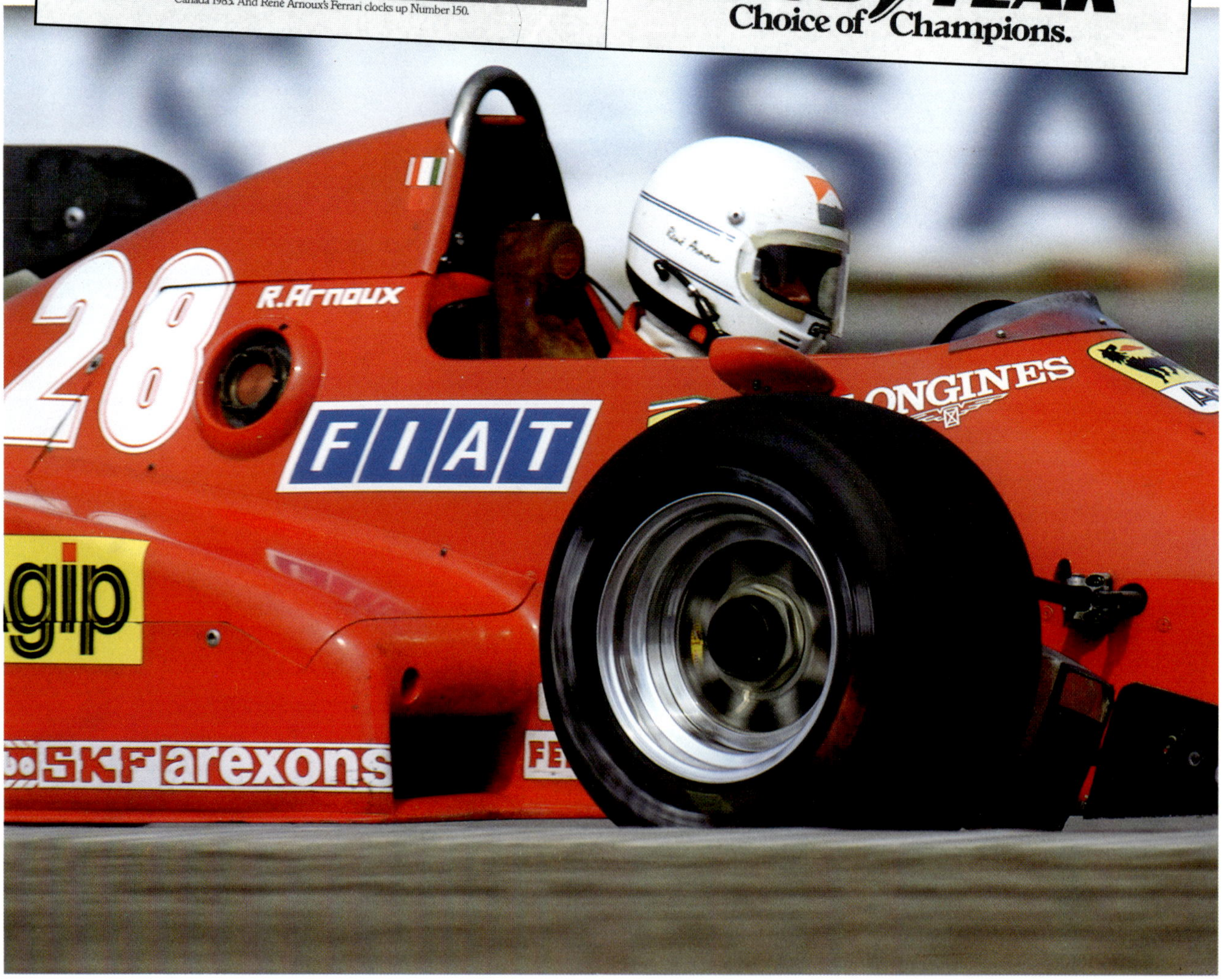
28
R.Arnoux
FIAT
LONGINES
agip
SKF arexons

Goodyear take leading roles in Dallas.

Congratulations to Keke Rosberg and the Williams team on winning last Sundays Grand Prix.

And our thanks to Ferrari, Lotus and the other Williams car on giving Goodyear the first four places.

It's from our experience on the track that we've designed the NCT.

A low profile high performance tyre built to bring out the best in your car.

Like our tyres on the track, we think you'll be impressed with the results.

AUTOSPORT, JULY 12, 1984

35

When Keke Rosberg won the 1984 Dallas Grand Prix in the Williams FW09-Honda, the Goodyear success advertisement stressed the link between racing technology and the NCT range of road tyres...

was now really intensifying for a switch to radials, which was duly achieved, initially for wet-weather tyres only, for 1984. However, there were only two wins waiting in a year when the McLaren-TAGs swept the board to establish a new record for a single season with 12 victories out of 16 races on Michelin radials and Nelson Piquet's Brabham-BMW scored two more on the French tyres.

Nevertheless, the two races which fell to Goodyear were truly commanding successes. In the Belgian Grand Prix at Zolder, Michele Alboreto's Ferrari 126C4 qualified on pole position and led every lap to beat Derek Warwick's Michelin-shod Renault RE50 into second place, while under a sweltering Texas summer sun Keke Rosberg dodged every hazard to score the first victory for the fledgling Williams-Honda alliance in the only championship race to be held in Dallas.

Top left: **Three-way split. Richie Ginther, Niki Lauda and René Arnoux all feature in this Goodyear spread, having respectively scored the first, 100th and 150th F1 victories on the tyres from the Akron company.**

Left: **René Arnoux scored his second victory of the 1983 season with a strong performance in the German Grand Prix at Hockenheim in the Ferrari 126C3.**

Niki Lauda wins the 1985 Dutch Grand Prix at Zandvoort, his last victory before his permanent retirement.

Jack Brabham, Leo Mehl and press officer Barry Griffin enjoy a cup of tea in the Goodyear motorhome. The Longines timing screen suggests that practice for this 1985 race is already under way!

The French company pulled out of F1 at the end of that season, so Goodyear returned to provide tyres for the World Champion McLaren squad for 1985, consolidating its position by at last making the switch to dry-weather radial rubber, which had been raced experimentally for the first time some seven years earlier on Patrick Tambay's McLaren M26 during the British Grand Prix at Brands Hatch.

McLaren Chief Designer John Barnard, working in conjunction with the team's two highly talented drivers Alain Prost and Niki Lauda, quickly adapted its cars to perform competitively on Goodyear's products and two more Drivers' World Championship titles were added in 1985 and '86. These both fell to Prost, thereby earning Goodyear the distinction of supplying its first 'back to back' World Champion driver. That feat in itself had not been achieved since Jack Brabham won the 1959 and '60 titles at the wheel of a Cooper-Climax.

1985 Alain Prost McLaren – Tag

Alain Prost won the first of his three championships in 1985. In his career to date the Frenchman has accumulated a staggering 44 Grand Prix victories – 28 of them on Goodyear tyres.

Marlboro
2
Shell
Shell
GOODYEAR
GOODYEAR

Lotus mechanics work hard to change the Goodyears on Johnny Dumfries's Lotus-Renault during the 1986 Brazilian Grand Prix at Rio.

The '86 championship battle turned out to be a sensational three-way affair between Williams-Honda team-mates Mansell and Piquet, and Alain Prost's McLaren-TAG. Mansell won five races, Prost and Piquet four apiece, but the title destiny was finally resolved during a spectacularly exciting finale at Adelaide in the last race of the year, the initiative passing between each of the three drivers during the course of the race before landing in Prost's lap.

From a tyre viewpoint, the 1986 Australian Grand Prix provided a reminder of how unpredictable the Formula 1 business can be, of how a chance technical failure/malfunction can jeopardise a season's effort. For Goodyear, it was a day when the wisdom of supporting a range of frontline teams was proved, for although two of the leading runners suffered freak tyre failures the championship was nevertheless clinched on Akron's products.

Mansell had qualified magnificently on pole position, and although he just got off the line first Ayrton Senna's Lotus 98T-Renault elbowed through into the lead at the second corner. Conscious that he should drive with the championship points situation in the forefront of his mind, Mansell dropped back to fourth by the end of the opening lap as Piquet and Keke Rosberg's McLaren-TAG also overtook him. This was Rosberg's last race before retirement from F1 and, determined to go out on a high note, he nipped through into the lead on the seventh lap and began to pull commandingly away from the field.

On lap 32 came the crucial and unexpected turn of fortune which helped decide the outcome of the race. As he was lapping Gerhard Berger's troubled Benetton-BMW, Prost bumped one of his front tyres against the Austrian's car, which prompted a slow deflation. The reigning champion stopped for a fresh set and resumed a distant fourth, now apparently out of the title equation.

Up to this stage, the Goodyear technicians had anticipated that most of their runners would have to make a routine tyre stop during the course of the race, but they changed their view after a close examination of the tyres which had come off the McLaren. Rosberg, meanwhile, continued to lead commandingly until lap 63 when he heard what he thought to be an expensive mechanical noise from the engine as he hurtled down the fastest section of the circuit.

GOODYEAR
EAGLE
GOOD YEAR
elf

1986 Alain Prost McLaren – Tag

These photos tell the story of Nigel Mansell's ill fortune in the 1986 Australian Grand Prix, when a deflated tyre *(above)* ruined the Englishman's chances of winning the World Championship. Mansell *(right)* walks dejectedly back to the pits while *(far right)* Alain Prost celebrates his second consecutive title.

Keke immediately slowed up, switched off the engine and pulled across to the side of the track. It was only once he had climbed out that he realised a rear tyre had delaminated and the noise had in fact been great strips of rubber banging against the McLaren's rear bodywork.

In the pit lane there was obviously some concern, even though Piquet and Mansell were now running first and third, separated by the fast-recovering Prost. Before any decision could be made Mansell suffered a failure almost identical to Rosberg's, just as the Williams-Honda was building up to more than 200 mph on the back straight while lapping Philippe Alliot's Ligier.

Alliot swerved out of the way as the debris began flying, while the Williams collapsed onto its left-rear suspension, lurching crazily from side to side. Mansell fought the car to a standstill in the escape road at the end of the long straight, but his championship prospects had evaporated in that haze of shredded rubber.

Now Piquet seemed on course for the race win that would clinch his third title, but Williams Chief Designer Patrick Head took the prudent decision to call him in for fresh tyres. Ironically, his existing ones were wearing perfectly well. The problems which had befallen both Mansell and Rosberg were chance malfunctions, failures which can occasionally afflict any highly stressed elements – be they tyres or other components – employed in fielding a front-running machine in such a tremendously competitive environment as F1 motor racing.

Even so, at this stage Prost still did not believe he was going to win; his McLaren's fuel consumption computer was signalling that he was five litres short of the total required to reach the chequered flag. On other days, he admitted, he might have eased off into a 'conservation mode' but on this occasion he willed himself into believing that the computer was wrong and drove the rest of the race as quickly as he could.

His judgement was absolutely spot on! The computer was delivering an inaccurate message. He finished ahead of Piquet to clinch his second World Championship in a row after one of the most breathtaking races of changing fortunes witnessed in living memory.

Throughout the 1987 season, the mix at the front of the field was much as before, with the Williams FW11B-Hondas now commanding pacemakers in a season which not only saw the turbo brigade restricted

Canon
Mobil
DENIM
ER'S

Mobil
Canon

The 1987 season was dominated by the Williams-Hondas of Nigel Mansell (leading) and Nelson Piquet.

GOOD YEAR
Tactel
ICI
POWERED BY
HONDA
Mobil 1
5
Canon
GOODYEAR
EAGLE
Tactel
ICI
Mobil 1
6
calma
DENIM
EAGLE
BP

1987 Nelson Piquet Williams – Honda

to 4-bar boost pressure for a second successive year, but their permitted fuel load reduced from 220 to 195 litres. The McLaren-TAG faded slightly, but still bagged three victories, while Maranello proved resurgent and returned to the victory circle after an absence of over two years, the longest barren period in the famous Italian team's history.

The architect of this victory, two and a half years after Alboreto had won the '85 German Grand Prix at the new Nürburgring, was none other than Gerhard Berger, the lanky Austrian who, a year earlier, had interrupted Goodyear's 1986 clean sweep with a win on Pirellis at the wheel of his Benetton-BMW. A fortnight after winning at Suzuka, Gerhard repeated that success with a similar runaway victory at Adelaide to clinch another milestone for Goodyear, its 200th Grand Prix triumph.

Another record was broken in 1987 when Alain Prost's victory in the Portuguese Grand Prix at Estoril brought the Frenchman's career total to 28 wins, beating the record of 27 which had stood to Jackie Stewart's credit since the Scot's retirement 14 years before. Alain had won only 11 of those races on Goodyears, but by the end of 1990 he had pushed his tally to a remarkable 44 victories, 28 of which had been achieved on Goodyears.

Left: **The Goodyear-shod Williams FW11Bs of Nelson Piquet and Nigel Mansell sit at the pit lane exit before the 1987 French Grand Prix.**

The 1988 Canadian Grand Prix at Montreal gets under way, with Alain Prost and Ayrton Senna leading the pack, as always, in their championship-winning McLaren MP4/4-Honda turbos.

Ayrton Senna, meanwhile, was busy establishing himself as one of the most dramatic new talents in the Grand Prix business, but Lotus mechanical frailty restricted him to six Grand Prix victories between 1985 and '87. In 1988 he formed an explosive new partnership with Prost in the McLaren-Honda line-up, these two highly motivated men helping to produce another Goodyear grand slam with 15 wins between them. The remaining triumph went to Berger's Ferrari at Monza, after Prost retired with engine trouble and Ayrton was eliminated in that celebrated moment when he tripped over Jean-Louis Schlesser's Williams in the closing stages of the race.

The end of 1988 closed a memorable chapter in F1 history with the finish of the turbo era, but the onset of the new naturally aspirated 3.5-litre regulations sustained Grand Prix racing's highly technical and competitive momentum. The next two seasons produced some absolutely dynamic racing which, all too frequently, got a little too close for comfort.

1988 Ayrton Senna McLaren – Honda

Overleaf: **A superb study of Ayrton Senna at work in the wet in the McLaren-Honda.**

Marlboro
12
Marlboro
HONDA
Shell
GOODYEAR

12
Shell

Left: **Prost and Senna in close company at Jerez during the '89 Spanish Grand Prix, which Ayrton won with Alain finishing third behind Gerhard Berger's Ferrari.**

Nigel Mansell won the first race of the new formula in the radical Goodyear-shod, John Barnard-designed Ferrari 640, distinguished by its ingenious electro-hydraulic gearchange system, while, at the other end of the year, Senna had his championship crown wrested back by Prost after a tense collision between the two McLaren-Hondas during the Japanese Grand Prix at Suzuka.

Suzuka continued to provide the backdrop to controversy 12 months later when the same two men were eliminated from the race, this time in a highly charged first-corner accident. By now Prost was at the wheel of a Ferrari, aiming to win a fourth title, but the mathematics were such that Senna became champion for the second time after parking his wrecked McLaren at the side of the circuit.

1989 Alain Prost McLaren – Honda

1990 Ayrton Senna McLaren – Honda

Overleaf: **Thierry Boutsen resisted every challenge to win the 1990 Hungarian Grand Prix for Williams, moving Goodyear ever closer to its 250th Grand Prix win.**

Ready for the off. Mansell's Ferrari 640 waits on the grid at Paul Ricard prior to the start of the 1989 French Grand Prix. The tyre warmers are to ensure that the rubber is as close to working temperature as possible before he sets off on his parade lap.

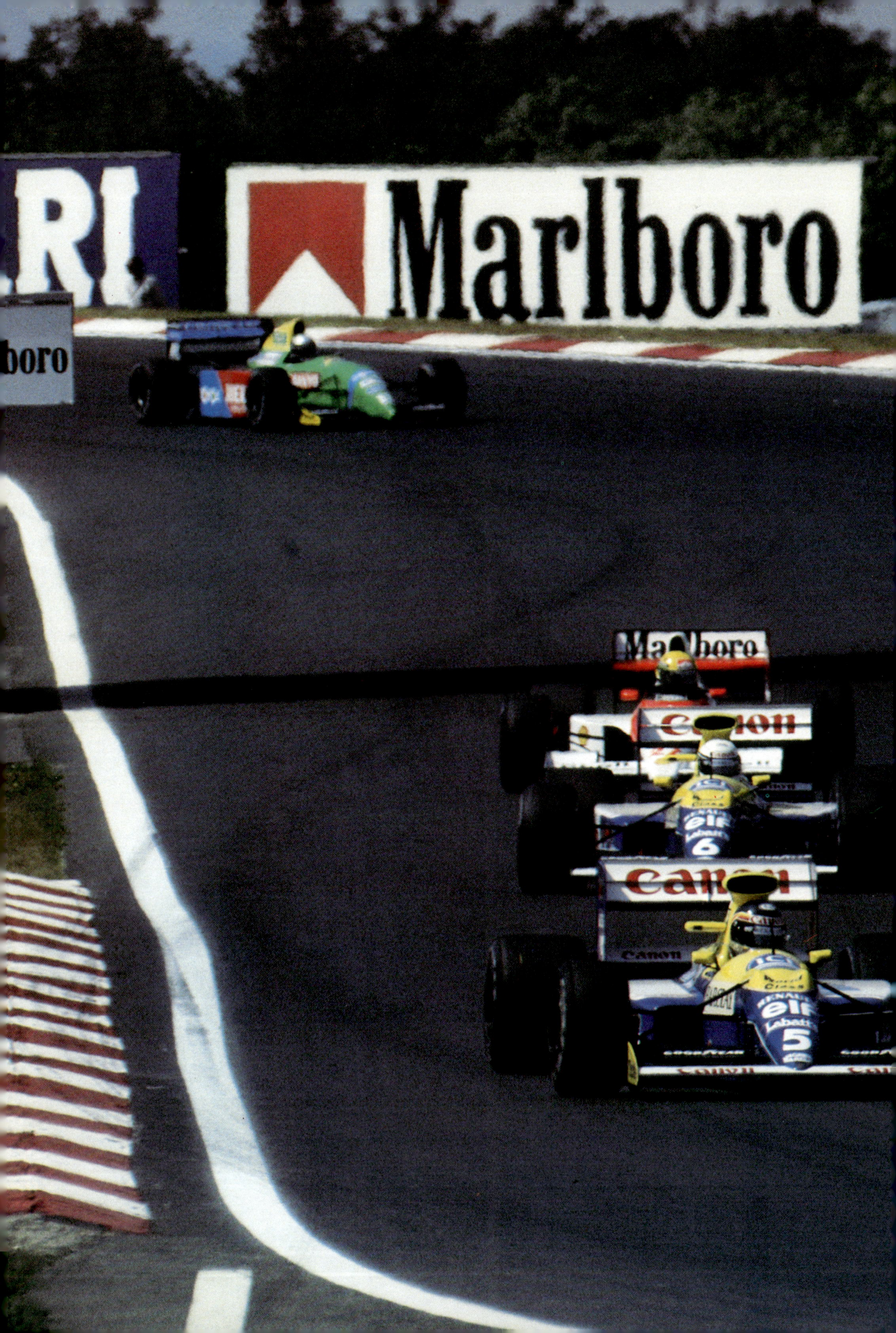

RI
Marlboro
lboro
Marlboro
canon
6
canon
5

GOODYEAR
Marlboro

Brazil 1991. On his way to his 28th and Goodyear's 250th Grand Prix win, Ayrton Senna leads the Williams pair Nigel Mansell and Riccardo Patrese with Jean Alesi's Ferrari in pursuit.

The 1990 season thus drew to a close with Nelson Piquet and Roberto Moreno scoring a 1-2 success in Japan, Berger having spun off at the scene of the Prost/Senna collision on the second lap and Mansell breaking his Ferrari's transmission in an over-zealous getaway from his pre-planned tyre stop. Nelson continued his renaissance a fortnight later in Adelaide, this time fending off a determined late-race charge from Nigel, who was having his final outing for the Prancing Horse.

Goodyear had now reached its 248th Grand Prix victory but, with Benetton making the switch to Pirelli for 1991, there was plenty of speculation that Akron might be made to sweat a little longer before the magical 250th win was notched up. However, with McLaren, Ferrari and Williams all continuing as Goodyear's prime runners into the new season, it was clear that 1991 would see the achievement of that momentous milestone. It was not a question of 'if', but merely of 'when'.

As things turned out, the issue was settled by the end of the first two races thanks to Ayrton Senna's stupendous form in the McLaren MP4/6, powered by Honda's totally new RA121E V12 engine. Ayrton led from start to finish in both Phoenix and Brazil and, although dire gearbox problems at Interlagos made him seem vulnerable to a late charge by Riccardo Patrese's Williams FW14, he hung on in fine style to chalk up an emotional first home win.

As McLaren number one took the chequered flag in front of the São Paulo crowd, so Senna scored the 28th Grand Prix victory of his career, moving ahead of Jackie Stewart in the all-time winners' stakes. Goodyear's 250th Grand Prix win was also in the bag and, appropriately, the power for that success came from Honda, the very people who had secured Goodyear's maiden victory in Mexico City just over 25 years earlier!

Canon
Marlboro

GOODYEAR

250

GRAND PRIX WINS

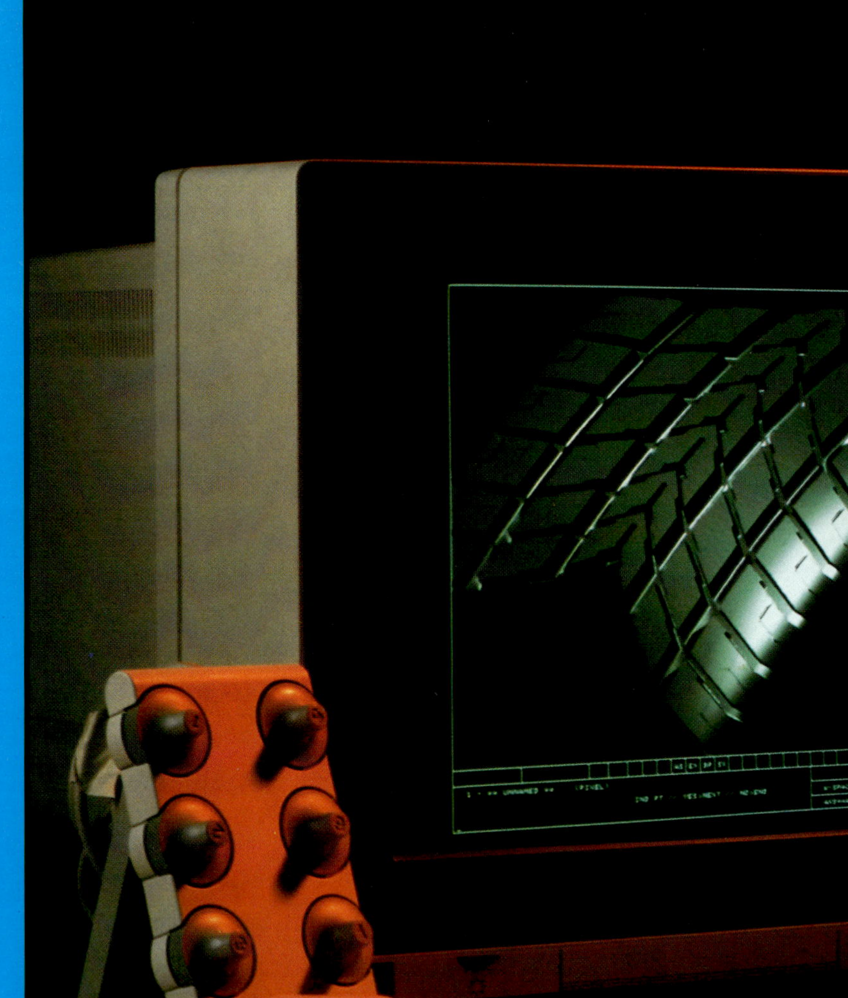

The Evolution
the

4

# of Technology

Jack Brabham's 1966 Brabham-Repco showing off its cross-ply racing tyres developed at Bushbury, Wolverhampton by the design team headed by Walt deVinney.

The development of racing tyre technology holds the ultimate key to the success or failure of a Grand Prix car design. The effectiveness of that elliptical contact patch between the tyre and track surface can make the difference between a winning performance and a disappointing mid-field showing. That's not to say that outstanding tyres can transform a second-rate car into a potential winner, but the performance of a highly competitive chassis package can certainly be detuned if it has to run on tyres which are less than fully competitive.

When Goodyear first appeared on the Grand Prix stage in 1964 it was breaking into a monopoly which had been enjoyed by the British Dunlop company since 1959. Throughout much of the 1½-litre Formula 1, between 1961 and '65, Dunlop was able to dictate the pace of tyre development – at a rate which was extremely modest by comparison with what was to come after Goodyear and Firestone pitched their hats into the ring. With sports car racing enjoying an international status every bit the equal of that of Grand Prix single-seaters, it was quite understandable that Dunlop's products were tailored to deal with the heaviest cars in the most gruelling conditions that could be anticipated.

It was only to be expected that racing tyres developed to sustain a Ferrari sports-prototype, weighing in the region of 2000 lb, around Le Mans for 24 hours at a maximum speed of 180 mph would be well within their capability on a Lotus, Cooper or Ferrari single-seater – tipping the scales at barely two-thirds that figure – running a two-hour Grand Prix with maximum speeds only touching 160 mph. It is a matter of history that Jim Clark's Lotus 25 completed four consecutive Grands Prix in the summer of '63, *en route* to the Scot's first World Championship title, on the same set of Dunlop covers.

Two decades later, dramatic technical progress would result in a powerful breed of turbocharged F1 cars developing almost twice as much aerodynamic downforce as that tiny Lotus's total weight, so it is hardly surprising that the demands placed on racing tyres changed almost beyond imagination.

When Goodyear arrived on the F1 scene, racing tyres were relatively tall and narrow. They were all manufactured from cross-ply construction and this methodology was retained by Akron for the ensuing 19 years. The complete casing of these tyres was constructed from cross-ply nylon cords, with every ply – or layer – of the tyre containing around thirty cords per inch, arranged in four-ply fashion.

The whole package was enveloped in a rubber compound to prevent the cords from rubbing together and creating unwanted friction within the tyre. The plies were laid at an angle to endow the tyre with maximum strength under hard braking and a wire bead was provided to help retain the cover on its wheel rim.

Three separate processes were involved in the manufacture of a cross-ply racing tyre. After the carcass had been completed, the tread was drawn through a die to a predetermined shape, after which it was attached to the carcass on a special machine. The beads were inserted into a setting ring on the outside of a drum, then the plies were all run onto this drum at various angles with the beads finally brought together against the drum. The plies themselves were turned up around the bead, a process which allowed the bead to be secured to the carcass, then two more plies were attached before the tread was finally added.

The tread compounds were applied to a thickness of between 0.2 in. and 0.4 in. across the tread, increasing to between 0.3 in. and 0.6 in. on the heavily stressed shoulders of the tyre. As the competitive tempo of Grand Prix racing increased over the years, the choice and make-up of the compound became one of the most crucial elements contributing to the successful performance of an individual tyre.

Goodyear's chemists rose to the challenge, basing their compounds on a complex blend of more than fifty different ingredients. In general terms, however, the ingredients can be grouped into five broad categories: polymers, fillers, oils, accelerators and sulphurs. These materials, all having varying physical characteristics, are mixed together at specific levels in order to obtain particular physical properties.

For example, the ingredients used in an earthmover tyre tread compound are significantly different from those required for a racing tyre. Although it is extremely difficult to grasp, rubber compounding in the area of racing tyre development has gradually become so complex that individual compounds are formulated for specific types of cars, specific tracks and, in many cases, specific wheel positions.

A polymer, or elastomer, is the basic ingredient in any rubber compound. Common polymers used in racing tyres include natural rubber, styrene butadiene rubber and poly butadiene rubber. Each polymer has its own unique properties and, accordingly, is chosen for a particular application. By the end of the 1980s, polymer science had become so sophisticated that it had become possible to manufacture unique polymers which provided a predetermined set of physical properties. This development work allowed the rubber compounder to obtain physical properties that were not previously attainable using conventional elastomers.

Fillers are those ingredients used to reinforce the polymer and impart certain physical properties and processing characteristics. The most commonly used filler is carbon black, although fine particle mineral pigments are used in some applications. Hundreds of types of carbon black are marketed, and are chosen by their particle size and structure in order to meet certain service demands. Carbon black reinforcement gives tyres their black appearance.

Oils are added to compound formulations in order to allow processability as well as to obtain certain physical properties. In order to mix a compound and properly incorporate the carbon black, oils must be added to provide lubrication between polymer chains. Even after mixing, oils are essential to the extruding and handling capability of rubber components. As a general classification, these oils can be grouped into paraffinic, napthenic and aromatic categories.

Accelerators are employed to enhance the formation of sulphur bonds during the curing process, during which the rubber compound is subjected to heat and pressure, forming chemical crosslinks between the polymer chains. It is this process which determines the ultimate physical properties of the rubber compound. As their name suggests, accelerators speed up bond formation during the curing cycle.

Because of the tremendous number of raw materials which have become available to the rubber compounder, the possible combinations of ingredients are almost infinite. Since there are no infallible mathematical formulae to determine physical properties, rubber compounding is part science and part art. Technology has increased Goodyear's choice of available polymers over the years, at the same time raising the company's level of understanding, but individual creativity

Slick tyres were regarded with some suspicion at the time this photo was taken in 1971, but soon they were to prove their superiority over 'intermediate' treaded designs.

and experience inevitably remain the key factors behind the success achieved by a rubber compounder.

Controlling internal heat build-up is another crucial consideration facing the tyre compounders, for an underheated tyre will not generate optimum grip, while an overheated carcass will eventually lose grip, blister and possibly even break up altogether. Goodyear is able to make the compounds softer or harder as required by varying the proportion of oil used, and the way in which the composition is mixed.

In the days of cross-ply covers, tyre construction design had to be tuned to the demands of individual cars, and this was, in effect, one of the main functions of the intensive tyre test sessions which increasingly became a feature of the F1 landscape in the 1970s and '80s. As knowledge and experience were gained, the tyre engineers gradually developed a more focused view of compounding as the precise mix came to be dictated by the known demands of particular circuits and their effects on the car's roadholding.

The construction of the carcass steadily became the most important priority, for the spring rate of the tyre wall itself is dictated by the loads it has to sustain in a downwards and sideways direction. The spring rate of a cross-ply tyre could frequently be varied by altering the angles at which the layers of carcass fabric were wrapped, and the type and number of cords employed per inch round its circumference.

In 1971 Goodyear introduced its first F1 slicks and, as Leo Mehl recalls, there was tremendous resistance in Grand Prix circles to their adoption. This was not entirely unexpected, since Akron had encountered exactly the same reaction when it started remaking the Indy car tread pattern in the late 1960s.

'I guess to explain how slicks actually developed, it's necessary to understand why the tread design was on racing tyres in the first place,' says Mehl. 'To begin with, race tyres for road courses in America were just modified street tyres. There was also an important commercial and advertising link; there was a strong attempt to keep a tread pattern with a traditional appearance. However, it soon became obvious that the cornering forces were directly related to the number of square inches of rubber gripping the road. Hence, eight square inches of rubber were better than six...

Goodyear's cross-ply rain tyre photographed at the 1976 Japanese Grand Prix at Mount Fuji whcrc James Hunt clinched the World Championship at the wheel of his McLaren M23.

'As race tyre development proceeded, so speeds increased dramatically. Speed creates heat which, traditionally, has become the most frightening enemy of a racing tyre. The most suitable carcass material from which to manufacture racing tyres is nylon; it's well suited for high speed and heat. But at around 350–400°F nylon melts.

'It really isn't a big problem on a racing tyre if the tread area blisters. The tyre goes out of balance, the driver feels the vibration and duly stops. The biggest worry is that tyres will reach the melting-point of their nylon carcass, so the grooves on the original tyres were really for cooling purposes. In the drivers' minds, however, the tread pattern equated to grip and traction. Although this was once probably true, improvements in the chemistry of rubber and compounding had changed all this by 1971 and, with slick technology, the treads had more grip and ran cooler.

'But in 1970/71 the drivers all equated slicks in their own mind to tyres which had worn out. Slicks meant "slippery" to them. People like Dan Gurney, Bruce McLaren and Denny Hulme had become convinced about slicks at Indy, which helped their acceptance in F1. But, in fact, for several seasons, we kept "intermediate" tread designs around to satisfy the diehards!'

By the mid-1970s, the Goodyear F1 involvement was becoming ever more sophisticated. The 1975–77 Vehicle Dynamics Programme involved the use of Goodyear-designed and -built equipment consisting of load and displacement transducers affixed to all four corners of the car, fore and aft accelerometers and steering angle transducers.

Typical construction of a modern Goodyear radial tyre. The cords running across from bead to bead, at right angles to the direction of travel, are the key to the radial's reduced tread distortion under load when compared with a cross-ply tyre.

The information provided was collected on a cassette and translated into a graphic display which illustrated every function, every element of a car's behaviour over a given lap. With the driver also subsequently being called upon to add comments on the car's behaviour indicated on the graph which had been produced, the chassis engineers began to reach a point where they were able to integrate the requirements of suspension and aerodynamic performance with that of the tyre development programme.

By 1984, Goodyear had accumulated sufficient technical knowledge to embark on the fresh challenge of manufacturing a radial racing tyre. The fundamental difference between a cross-ply and a radial cover is that the latter has the cords running from bead to bead across the tyre crown at right angles to the direction of travel, improving pliability and ride comfort. Stability is conferred by 'breakers' – a belt of cords which run round the tyre circumference, beneath the tread or rolling surface. These are usually made from thin, flexible and tough steel wire and restrict the lateral stretching of the tread during cornering.

This breaker section is made from several layers of cord laid at a slight angle to the tyre wall, varying from about 15 to 20 degrees, to create resistance to deflection during cornering and, to some extent, can be altered to dictate tyre behaviour on different circuits.

The practical performance benefits offered by a radial tyre include reduced tread distortion under load, although this was initially achieved at the expense of increased sidewall distortion. Its construction theoretically offers greater flexibility and straightline stability, greater cornering force, better traction and improved braking capability. Steering is generally more responsive on radial rubber, although these tyres tend to offer less progressive warning of imminent loss of adhesion when operating close to their limit.

Radial tyres also demonstrate much less of a tendency to 'grow' through centrifugation at high speed than their cross-ply counterparts. With the technology of chassis aerodynamics demanding a much more consistent ride height than ever before with the introduction of the 'flat-bottom' F1 regulations at the start of 1983, the pressure mounted even more for Goodyear to go radial.

Leo Mehl explains the factors which made Goodyear hold off for so

Right: **Hand-cutting the grooves on wet-weather tyres prior to the start of the rain-soaked 1984 Monaco Grand Prix.**

Nigel Mansell's Lotus 95T led the 1984 Monaco Grand Prix in the wet, before spinning into a barrier, on the debut of Goodyear's radial construction F1 rain tyres.

long in developing and introducing its own radial F1 tyre: 'First of all, our initial attempts to make radial race tyres were not successful. The breakaway characteristics were too sudden and unpredictable. In addition, it was a fact of life that such a switch in manufacturing technique would render totally obsolete the biggest race tyre manufacturing factory in the world. All our equipment would be of no further use. In addition, there was no doubt that radial tyres would be extremely expensive to manufacture.

'Radial tyres demand precision. While we had the best bias [cross-ply] tyre manufacturing machines in the world, the decision would have to be made to design a totally new machine, from scratch, simply for racing tyres. Consequently, it was logical to delay this as long as possible.

'By the early 1980s, although Renault was running with Michelin radials, we hadn't got beaten yet. In fact, with Ferrari, we seemed quite competitive with our bias tyre.

'But we were not complacent in any way. We knew we couldn't keep full-scale bias and radial development programmes going at the same time. I guess what finally did the trick was when it rained during an untimed practice session at the 1983 Detroit Grand Prix – not only was Michelin much faster than we were, but so was Pirelli, on cars which were normally slower. As I recall, we were about seven seconds off the pace, so there remained no further doubt that we had to go radial.

'The pressure then began from the teams, with our old friend Enzo Ferrari taking a personal interest in our progress. We introduced our radial rain tyre the following May in Monaco after constant requests from Ferrari. There was also the consideration that our new Chairman, Bob Mercer, was going to attend that event!'

One of the most ambitious and exciting resources Goodyear can now call upon in the development of its racing tyres is what's termed the 'Predictive Testing Race Circuit Simulation System', a computer tool which is based at the Akron racing headquarters. It is one of many programmes geared to predictive testing at the computer work-stations, offering the possibility of achieving final confirmation of a tyre's potential with the minimum of actual track testing.

The objectives of the programme are to optimise a tyre for a specific circuit and to assist the company in engineering the most suitable tyre

Goodyear's NCT 2 is typical of the contemporary breed of radial road tyre which owes much of its technical heritage to the lessons learned on the race track.

for tracks which are not available for pre-event testing, such as Monaco or Phoenix which are only open for the Grand Prix weekend itself.

The input data for the computer programme can be grouped into three categories: the race circuit itself, the competing vehicle and the tyre concerned.

Circuit input parameters consist of two elements, the first of which is a complete, three-dimensional projection of the track's geometry. On an incremental basis, the programme input includes grade, elevations, track lengths, widths, turn radii and banking angle.

The next part of the input is the frictional coefficient of the track surface itself, while vehicle input requires very precise definition, relying on contributions from F1 designers to provide accurate engineering information. Of major concern for the computer model are mass, weight distribution, height of the centre of gravity and the geometry of the car's wheelbase and track. Also taken into account are the power characteristics of the engine plus aerodynamic drag and downforce.

Goodyear's prime concern is the performance of the tyres, and the tyre parameters – essentially the amount of fore/aft and lateral force which the tyre will generate under conditions of varying load, slip angle and camber – consequently form a major part of the input.

The computer simulation starts in the middle of the corner, at the point where the vehicle is under maximum cornering conditions. From that point the computer works backwards on an incremental basis, generating the racing line using the maximum deceleration potential of the tyre/vehicle system. The computer then works forward from the corner using the maximum acceleration possible. This method continues from corner to corner until a continuous convergent racing line is generated. This enables the computer to produce the ideal racing line round the entire circuit.

As output data from the model, we have an overall lap time and racing distance while, in addition, a station-by-station output – approximately every 10 to 20 feet – provides elapsed time and distances as well as the velocity and longitudinal and lateral acceleration forces imposed on the tyre, all of which are available on a digital or graphical read-out.

Goodyear's circuit map consists of over 500 individual track increments, each with its own physical description. In essence, we have

created a finite element model of the track geometry.

In assessing the progress made by Goodyear over the past four decades of international motor racing, it is crucial to bear in mind that dramatic progress has not just been made in manufacturing the tyres themselves. The design and building of the equipment to fulfil this task is in a constant state of evolution to this very day.

Leo Mehl: 'When race tyre manufacturing began at Goodyear on a serious note in the early 1960s, it was immediately found that the existing building equipment and machines would have to be modified to accept the newly required sizes and profiles. Initially bias truck tyre equipment was used, but size became an immediate problem. The tall and narrow truck tyre machines were OK for a short time, but once racing tyres were changed to incorporate shorter sidewall lengths for increased cornering stability, we had to make a change.

'Fortunately, Goodyear has its own machine design department, and there is no doubt that, without their help, we would never have maintained our technical edge over the competition all these years. It's easy enough to dream up new ideas for tyres. The tough part is converting the ideas into actual tyres – not just any tyres, but the most precision-built tyres in the industry.

'Every tyre has a critical role to play, but a racing tyre on the right-front wheel of a Grand Prix car at 200 mph in a 3G corner has to be perfect every time. The primary contribution of an expertly designed tyre-building machine is not to make the odd tyre perfect, but to make every tyre perfect. We remain totally committed to this day to our expert builders, as well as the equipment, to achieve this...'

The Link

5

with Road Tyres

The entrance to Goodyear's European Technical Centre at Colmar-Berg, Luxembourg.

The belief that Grand Prix racing improves the breed is an absolute, unshakeable tenet behind Goodyear's continuing commitment to a Formula 1 programme. In terms of accelerating the development of passenger tyres, both as original equipment and for the replacement market, Goodyear's technical progress has been enhanced considerably by its racing programmes.

Leo Mehl: 'We as a company also get worthwhile technical spin-off in any areas where tyres are subject to high heat conditions, such as aircraft tyres, and any area in which it is necessary to learn about wet-weather traction, again for trucks and aircraft. In addition, we have made improvements in the technology we have used for manufacturing the tyres – in other words, in terms of the machinery and building equipment. That sort of advance in technology applies to any sort of tyre.'

When it comes to tracing the path of direct racing development influencing road car tyres, Mehl has no difficulty in being very specific indeed: 'Take the "gator back" tread design which we used as our wet-weather F1 tyre back in 1981. That tread pattern really worked well. It was the initial biased rain tyre, incorporating a distinctive directional tread for maximum water evacuation, running against Michelin radials, and was very respectable indeed. Later you could see it as the most successful high-performance road tyre in America – as the Eagle VR – fitted to quick cars like Corvettes and so on. That is a definite example of a racing development which is there for all to see.

'In the radial passenger and truck tyre areas we made a number of other developments with exciting new materials. They have all definitely contributed to the overall pool of technical knowledge within the company as a whole. Since we made the switch to radial technology, the racing department has probably been making a better technical contribution to the company than ever before.'

Of course, it is important to remember that technical quantum leaps forward do not often occur in the area of tyre development. 'Things don't happen that way,' explains Mehl, 'but I think the progress we have made has helped American car manufacturers to really appreciate what a tyre can do for their vehicles. Our products are now so good that the average road car comes out of the showroom on a set of radials and the owner will need only one replacement set, at perhaps 30,000–40,000

Under-track photography enables Goodyear engineers to form an accurate picture of how the various tread patterns perform at high speed. *Left:* **The photo image reveals that the tread pattern is dispersing the water satisfactorily.**

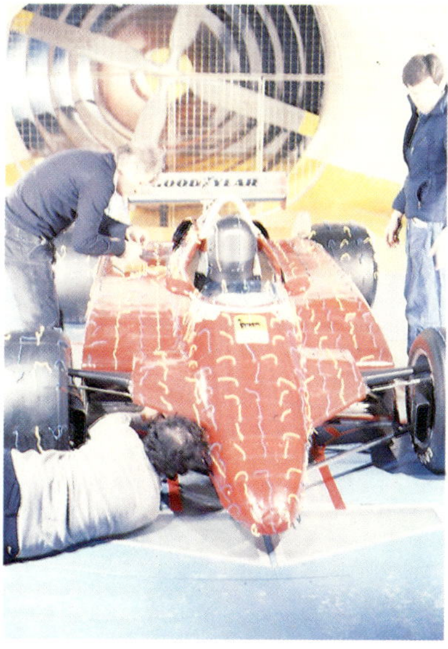

Extensive wind tunnel work being carried out with a Ferrari 126C2 to determine the effect of the tyres on the overall aerodynamic efficiency of the car.

miles, to see out the life of his car.

'There used to be a time when the original equipment wouldn't last near as long, so perhaps he would use five sets, rather than two, during the life of the car. This is one of the reasons that tyre business in the United States is contracting. The replacement market is reducing because the tyres are better than they were ten years ago. And racing programmes have contributed to this.'

Fuel consumption is another area where improvements in tyre

Lateral and radial forces being analysed on a computer at one of Goodyear's technical centres.

technology can produce seemingly marginal, but none the less crucial, benefits. In the USA car designers are faced with having to come to terms with the CAFE – Corporate Average Fuel Economy – regulations, a set of mandatory rules laid down by the government which require each manufacturer's complete range of cars to average out at a given fuel consumption figure.

In reality, if a manufacturer has a 7-litre gas-guzzler in its line-up, it could well kill the entire range as it will prove extremely difficult for the smaller-engined cars to balance this out. What makes this considerably more serious is that the fines for failing to meet these requirements are so enormous that no efforts are spared to ensure that the requisite consumption figures are achieved.

That may seem a long way from being a tyre maker's problem. However, when the tyre maker is approached by an original equipment customer and told, 'We need a tyre with less rolling resistance for good fuel consumption, but we want excellent traction as well and good mileage as far as wear is concerned,' then it immediately becomes his problem. Many manufacturers have been asking for wider tyres, which improve the car's cosmetic appearance and have larger 'footprints' to cope with the new demands of handling which have, particularly in the USA, become a recent priority.

For many years, Jackie Stewart was actively involved in the development of Goodyear road tyres. He sees the development of road car tyre

An aerial view of one of Goodyear's European test track facilities, showing the wide variety of circuit configurations available.

technology, especially on the American market, as having its roots partly in the aftermath of the fuel crises of the 1970s and early '80s. He also believes that competitive and imaginative compounding technology, developed from Goodyear's F1 participation, provided a significant key in responding to the road car challenge.

'In years gone by, the American motor industry never built a car which really handled well in the European sense of the word,' he contends. 'Then suddenly the second fuel crisis came along and imported cars began to make major inroads into the US market because they were smaller, lighter and, of course, had better fuel consumption.

'The US manufacturers' reaction to this new competition was to put bigger wheels and tyres on their reduced-size models in an attempt to improve handling. But those wider wheels and tyres meant more rolling resistance; it is more difficult to push the car along when it has more rubber on the road and is generating more surface friction. So people said, "OK, we'll make a harder compound, therefore you'll have a wider car and better mileage on tyre wear yet still have good fuel consumption." That worked until the rain came and then the hard compound slipped all over the place as it had no grip. It proved extremely difficult to produce a tyre design and compound which worked together as an acceptable compromise.

'I learned from the work I did with Goodyear that this is one of the main issues which was addressed, and many of the compounders who were working in the racing department are now compounders working on original-equipment passenger car tyres, trying to get that rolling resistance factor married to footprint, adhesion and styling. That has been an enormously important element in the tyre maker's challenge to satisfy not only the car makers, but also government requirements. So these engineers have been exercised to the limits of their ability in this gymnasium which we call motor sport. They are fitter, stronger, more agile and constantly on the look-out for better alternatives, keeping in mind all the latest, constantly changing requirements.'

Victory is the prime consideration behind Goodyear's Grand Prix racing effort, but while the company certainly relishes its success on the tracks, the long-term technical benefits for road tyres provide the ultimate pay-off.

Jackie Stewart carried out as much road tyre testing for Goodyear after his retirement from the cockpit as he did race tyre testing during his career. This sequence of shots shows him during the course of development work at the wheel of a Chevrolet Corvette sports coupé.

Putting a Ferrari flat-12 Testa Rossa through its paces at the Luxembourg test track.

Leo Mehl puts the pace of improvement into sharp perspective by affectionately recalling a tale involving Jochen Rindt during the summer of 1968: 'It was the free day between final qualifying and the race at the French Grand Prix at Rouen. Jochen had planted his Brabham-Repco on pole position, but he wasn't very confident about it lasting more than a few laps on the Sunday, so he took me off to Paris to do the full tourist bit on the Saturday. We came home pretty late in Jochen's Porsche 911, running absolutely flat out on the road, when I started to become worried about this clunking sound.

'I said to Jochen, "What on earth's wrong?" and he just shrugged, replying, "It's those bloody tyres again, they're always chunking like that..." I looked over to the instruments and the speedometer was off the clock at what looked like 130 mph, then there was another big clunk and I shouted, "Jochen, stop the car!"

'So we pulled over and got out and, would you believe, the whole inside shoulder had come away. I said, "Good grief!"...or something like that, while Rindt simply stood there muttering, "I've tried every tyre in the world and they're all junk." I should point out that these were not Goodyears, incidentally!

'I suddenly realised that these guys drove like that as a matter of routine, so I went back and enquired whether we had anything up to that sort of job, only to find that we had nothing really rated for more than 100 mph. Now there are any number of tyres rated for 125 mph!

'Going on from that, it's worth considering our partnership with Ferrari. It's not merely a racing obligation, it's a high-performance tyre commitment to produce a tyre for whatever Maranello thinks up next. For a GTO, or an F40, or whatever, which can run 210 mph but which owners still want to drive round their local neighbourhood streets, perhaps kerb it, then go out and drive it quickly again after it's been sitting in their garage for a month. It has to display adequate ride qualities at 55 mph, yet be capable of being run at 185 mph at the other end of the scale...

'That's what racing enables us to find out all about.'

There could be no clearer evidence of the direct transfer of technology from the track to the road than the striking similarity between the tread patterns of the current Eagle F1 rain tyre *(left)* **and the high-performance Eagle ZR road tyre** *(below left)*.

GOODYEAR

250

GRAND PRIX WINS

6

Formula 1 Testing

Right: **The Lotus 72s of Brian Henton and Ronnie Peterson in the pit lane at Silverstone during pre-British Grand Prix testing, 1975.**

The good old days. Bert Baldwin rides on the engine cover of Dan Gurney's Eagle, studying tyre tread distortion at Goodwood, 1967.

Although several of the major Grand Prix constructors have separate, self-contained test teams available throughout the season, Goodyear's International Racing Division has to meet the tyre requirements of an ongoing test programme within the logistical framework of its race service commitments. Apart from posing a considerable logistical challenge, this keeps the engineering personnel working under strong pressure throughout the Formula 1 season, for progress in race tyre design is, as Leo Mehl emphasises, a gradual process rather than the result of 'blinding flash' inspiration.

Throughout the European season, the Formula One Constructors' Association schedules a series of official test sessions for the Formula 1 teams, and it is at these sessions that most of Goodyear's test and development work is carried out. Weather conditions in Europe inevitably restrict off-season testing. For many years up until the early 1980s, the early-season South African Grand Prix at Kyalami was preceded by a week or so of official tyre testing. With good weather in South Africa almost guaranteed, it provided an ideal opportunity for Goodyear to run through a consistent development programme in order to evaluate new compounds and constructions for the coming season.

As the 1991 World Championship opened, the bulk of Goodyear's test and development work was focused on three major contracted teams: McLaren, Ferrari and Williams. This trio of front-running outfits have the benefit of definitive contracts with Goodyear, not only providing for free tyre supply and service but also offering a retainer in exchange for the regular testing work they carry out.

The remainder of the Goodyear competitors receive their tyre supplies on a commercial basis, although Leo Mehl is quick to point out that the charges made go only a small part of the way towards defraying the enormous costs involved in operating a Grand Prix tyre programme.

A typical programme at one of the FOCA test sessions may involve one of the contracted teams agreeing to make available one of its two cars for tyre testing for, perhaps, two or three days. Inevitably, with competitive pressures as they are, events at a previous race may mean that it is not possible for the team to carry out its obligation. If a major chassis problem crops up, for example, it may mean that it has to duck out and concentrate on other elements of its cars' performance.

In such a case, Goodyear may request one of the other teams – outside the contracted three – to help out on test and development work. McLaren, Ferrari and Williams will inevitably benefit if Goodyear runs a specially organised tyre test for its own purposes, outside the FOCA schedule. For example, in 1990 Goodyear arranged a special test at the Hungaroring immediately following the Italian Grand Prix to evaluate the progress made with compounds and constructions in the month since the Hungarian Grand Prix. There was also an exclusive test at Donington, a session at Fiorano solely for Ferrari's benefit just prior to the Imola race, and another test at Imola during the week following the San Marino Grand Prix.

'Test sessions are crucial to our keeping the wolf from the door in terms of anticipating what the opposition might be likely to produce in

Jean Alesi paddles into the pit lane at the wheel of his Ferrari during F1 tyre tests at Estoril early in 1991. Rain or shine, there are always lessons to be learned for Goodyear from these crucial sessions working with the top Grand Prix teams.

the foreseeable future,' explains Tony Shakespeare. 'And we always tend to learn something, even if the weather is bad and it appears, to outsiders, to be a bit of a waste of time. As an example, our final pre-1991 season test at Estoril was largely spoiled by rain, yet we did gain some data which we believed would help us when it came to preparing our qualifying tyres for Phoenix, the first race of the year.

'In general terms, we never stop the development work, but the pace at which it progresses depends on the pressure from the opposition. If Pirelli start to push hard in 1991, then we might really have to pull out all the stops. But the process of development and improvement is continuous.'

Of course, while the effectiveness of qualifying rubber becomes a matter of absolute priority to all drivers during those two crucial, hour-long timed sessions during practice for a World Championship Grand Prix, it is the performance and durability of race rubber which becomes the most important item on the agenda at most of the test sessions. The seasoned and experienced Formula 1 driver knows full well that a *banzai* 'qualifying' lap, set on soft rubber, may produce a time which looks good in the columns of the specialist magazines when it comes to reports of individual tests. But the real worth of his car's performance is what lap times it can turn, consistently, running with a significant fuel load on the race tyres that he is going to use when it comes to competing in a Grand Prix on that very track. A rival team's performance can be enormously difficult to gauge accurately under the circumstances of a Goodyear tyre test – which is precisely the situation most competitors are keen to foster!

Goodyear's test programmes have come a long way since Leo Mehl, then one of the racing division's compounders, spent an intensive winter programme with Jack Brabham at Riverside in the early stages of the company's involvement. Shuttling back and forth between California and Akron, the team eventually finalised what it regarded as the optimum tyre for Jack's Tasman Championship programme and the gritty Australian departed from Los Angeles *en route* to Sydney with the latest set literally tucked under his arm.

When the 2.5-litre Tasman Brabham-Repco got to Sydney's Warwick Farm circuit, it simply flew away from the opposition on its new rubber, a real vindication of all that testing effort. However, these were early days for Goodyear's international racing involvement, a time when Dunlop ruled the roost and Firestone was just becoming a force to be reckoned with on the F1 front.

Today, with Goodyear established as the most consistently successful Formula 1 tyre supplier of all, test and development programmes continue to underpin the company's position. Tyre testing can be an unglamorous aspect of Grand Prix racing, taking place on empty circuits in front of deserted grandstands. But in Formula 1's academy, if the race is the examination, then the test session is the crucial homework. And Goodyear knows very well that nobody ever passed an exam without paying a great deal of attention to private study!

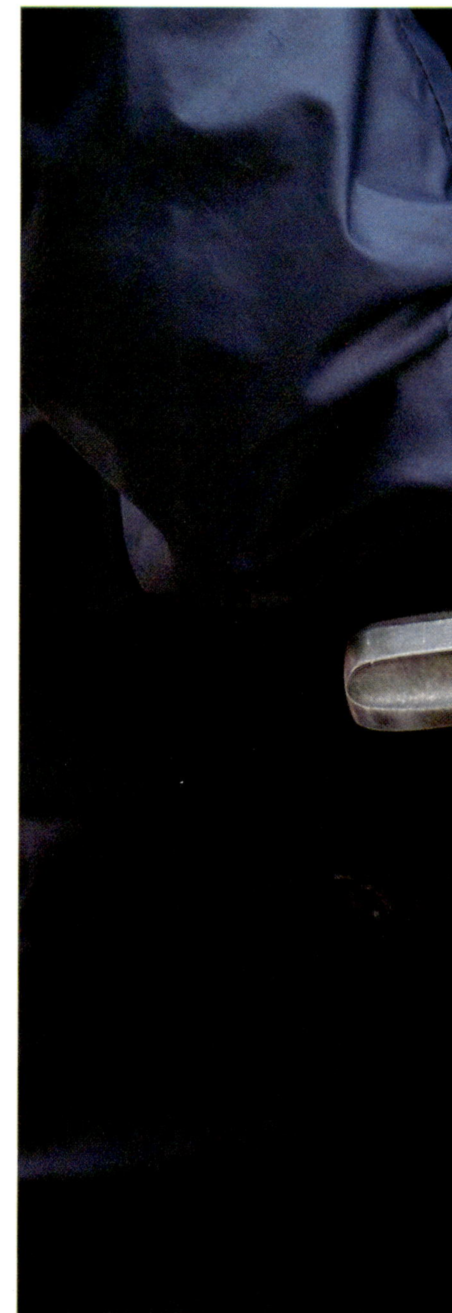

A Goodyear F1 technician with one of the tools of his trade, the thermometer used for monitoring operating temperatures across the surface of the tread.

THE VITAL CONNECTION

They call it "seat of the pants testing," it's the testing that no machine can ever take over because no computer can ever replace the vital connection between the seat of the pants and the human brain. When it comes to the crucial question of the "feel" of a tyre, whether it's a road tyre that is never going to go over 70 kph or a racing tyre that is designed to run at over 300, no instruments can give you the information that you can glean from a skilled test driver.

Today, testing is a more important part of the racing division's work than ever before and test sessions are held at all the major race tracks to develop tyres which will exactly suit the characteristics of that particular track. The dependence on feedback from the driver is just one similarity between the testing techniques used on the race track and those used on Goodyear's testing grounds like the one at the massive Goodyear International Test Centre at Colmar-Berg in Luxemburg.

The top racing drivers who carry out tests for Goodyear, like Mario Andretti and Niki Lauda, have the same approach to their job as the drivers on the company's tyre test fleet. They must take the tyre to the limits of its capability while at the same time assessing its characteristics and judging the effect on the car's handling. They must be able to make this assessment whilst driving the car at top speed, and then they must be able to report their findings clearly to the engineers when the drive is over.

Of course, the most important factor in race tyre testing is the stop watch. Lap times are measured in hundredths of seconds

11

Reproduction of a publicity hand-out titled *The Vital Connection* covering details of F1 testing with John Watson and the Brabham-Alfa Romeo team at Monza in 1978.

struction can no longer hold up and it fails. Obviously a safety factor is built into tyres so that they can be run safely on the road at their designated safe speeds, so even a road tyre with a designated safe speed of 180 kph will go far beyond that before it fails on the testing machine. Racing tyres are designed to run at over 320 kph so you can imagine that after designing and constructing a tyre testing machine which will take them to their failure speed the engineers have a lot of information to help them design machines to operate at lower speeds.

But, whatever you are testing—from tractor tyres at 16 kph to Formula One tyres at 320 kph—the machines can only tell you so much and there is still a requirement for that vital connection between the seat of the pants and the brain.

13

and a tyre which will make a car go a couple of tenths of a second faster per lap is a real achievement. For this reason, all race tyre test sessions are timed to a tenth of a second. Although the products will never be used for racing, the stopwatch has its part to play in road tyre tests too. When comparison tests are being made at Goodyear's Colmar-Berg centre, the time taken to go round the test circuit, with its selection of difficult bends, is a useful indicator and timing equipment measures every lap. The lap times provide a useful yardstick by which to compare the tyres and how they are coping with the problems which the track's selection of bends present.

Machines and recording devices are also an important part of test procedures and in this area the racers are learning from the road testers. The trend towards miniaturisation which is so much a part of modern technology has made it possible to make measuring devices much more compact and recorders which previously would only fit in the boot of a passenger car are now small enough to be carried on a Formula One car. Goodyear led the way in this development and has gained a great deal of knowledge about vehicle behaviour from its experiments with fully instrumented racing cars. It's a two-way traffic, however, because the strains placed on the measuring devices being operated at racing speeds have led to changes which have improved their dependability for normal testing.

There is one area, however, where both road and racing tyres have to leave the test tracks behind and come inside. That's destruction testing, where a tyre is deliberately taken to and beyond its limits of performance. Goodyear has a number of tyre testing machines which consist of large rotating wheels, called dynamometers, against which the test tyres are run. The wheel is driven at ever increasing speed until the tyre is turning at such a speed that its con-

GOODYEAR
250
GRAND PRIX WINS

1965-1991

	EVENT	VENUE	DATE	DRIVER	CAR
1	Mexican GP	*Mexico City*	24 October 1965	Richie Ginther	Honda RA272
2	French GP	*Reims*	3 July 1966	Jack Brabham	Brabham BT19-Repco
3	British GP	*Brands Hatch*	16 July 1966	Jack Brabham	Brabham BT19-Repco
4	Dutch GP	*Zandvoort*	24 July 1966	Jack Brabham	Brabham BT19-Repco
5	German GP	*Nürburgring*	7 August 1966	Jack Brabham	Brabham BT19-Repco
6	Monaco GP	*Monte Carlo*	7 May 1967	Denny Hulme	Brabham BT20-Repco
7	Belgian GP	*Spa-Francorchamps*	18 June 1967	Dan Gurney	Eagle T1G-Weslake
8	French GP	*Le Mans*	2 July 1967	Jack Brabham	Brabham BT24-Repco
9	German GP	*Nürburgring*	6 August 1967	Denny Hulme	Brabham BT24-Repco
10	Canadian GP	*Mosport Park*	27 August 1967	Jack Brabham	Brabham BT24-Repco
11	Belgian GP	*Spa-Francorchamps*	9 June 1968	Bruce McLaren	McLaren M7A-Ford
12	Italian GP	*Monza*	8 September 1968	Denny Hulme	McLaren M7A-Ford
13	Canadian GP	*Ste Jovite-Mt Tremblant*	22 September 1968	Denny Hulme	McLaren M7A-Ford
14	German GP	*Nürburgring*	3 August 1969	Jacky Ickx	Brabham BT26A-Ford
15	Canadian GP	*Mosport Park*	20 September 1969	Jacky Ickx	Brabham BT26A-Ford
16	Mexican GP	*Mexico City*	19 October 1969	Denny Hulme	McLaren M7A-Ford
17	South African GP	*Kyalami*	7 March 1970	Jack Brabham	Brabham BT33-Ford
18	Spanish GP	*Montjuich Park*	18 April 1971	Jackie Stewart	Tyrrell 003-Ford
19	Monaco GP	*Monte Carlo*	23 May 1971	Jackie Stewart	Tyrrell 003-Ford
20	French GP	*Paul Ricard*	4 July 1971	Jackie Stewart	Tyrrell 003-Ford
21	British GP	*Silverstone*	17 July 1971	Jackie Stewart	Tyrrell 003-Ford
22	German GP	*Nürburgring*	1 August 1971	Jackie Stewart	Tyrrell 003-Ford
23	Canadian GP	*Mosport Park*	19 September 1971	Jackie Stewart	Tyrrell 003-Ford
24	US GP	*Watkins Glen*	3 October 1971	François Cevert	Tyrrell 002-Ford
25	Argentine GP	*Buenos Aires*	23 January 1972	Jackie Stewart	Tyrrell 003-Ford
26	South African GP	*Kyalami*	4 March 1972	Denny Hulme	McLaren M19A-Ford
27	French GP	*Clermont-Ferrand*	2 July 1972	Jackie Stewart	Tyrrell 003-Ford
28	Canadian GP	*Mosport Park*	24 September 1972	Jackie Stewart	Tyrrell 003-Ford
29	US GP	*Watkins Glen*	8 October 1972	Jackie Stewart	Tyrrell 003-Ford
30	Argentine GP	*Buenos Aires*	28 January 1973	Emerson Fittipaldi	Lotus 72D-Ford
31	Brazilian GP	*Interlagos*	11 February 1973	Emerson Fittipaldi	Lotus 72D-Ford
32	South African GP	*Kyalami*	3 March 1973	Jackie Stewart	Tyrrell 006-Ford
33	Spanish GP	*Montjuich Park*	29 April 1973	Emerson Fittipaldi	Lotus 72E-Ford
34	Belgian GP	*Zolder*	20 May 1973	Jackie Stewart	Tyrrell 006-Ford
35	Monaco GP	*Monte Carlo*	3 June 1973	Jackie Stewart	Tyrrell 006-Ford
36	Swedish GP	*Anderstorp*	17 June 1973	Denny Hulme	McLaren M23-Ford
37	French GP	*Paul Ricard*	1 July 1973	Ronnie Peterson	Lotus 72E-Ford
38	British GP	*Silverstone*	14 July 1973	Peter Revson	McLaren M23-Ford
39	Dutch GP	*Zandvoort*	29 July 1973	Jackie Stewart	Tyrrell 006-Ford
40	German GP	*Nürburgring*	5 August 1973	Jackie Stewart	Tyrrell 006-Ford
41	Austrian GP	*Österreichring*	19 August 1973	Ronnie Peterson	Lotus 72E-Ford
42	Italian GP	*Monza*	9 September 1973	Ronnie Peterson	Lotus 72E-Ford
43	Canadian GP	*Mosport Park*	23 September 1973	Peter Revson	McLaren M23-Ford
44	US GP	*Watkins Glen*	7 October 1973	Ronnie Peterson	Lotus 72E-Ford
45	Argentine GP	*Buenos Aires*	13 January 1974	Denny Hulme	McLaren M23-Ford
46	Brazilian GP	*Interlagos*	27 January 1974	Emerson Fittipaldi	McLaren M23-Ford
47	South African GP	*Kyalami*	30 March 1974	Carlos Reutemann	Brabham BT44-Ford
48	Spanish GP	*Jarama*	28 April 1974	Niki Lauda	Ferrari 312B3
49	Belgian GP	*Nivelles*	12 May 1974	Emerson Fittipaldi	McLaren M23-Ford
50	Monaco GP	*Monte Carlo*	26 May 1974	Ronnie Peterson	Lotus 72E-Ford

	EVENT	VENUE	DATE	DRIVER	CAR
51	Swedish GP	*Anderstorp*	9 June 1974	Jody Scheckter	Tyrrell 007-Ford
52	Dutch GP	*Zandvoort*	23 June 1974	Niki Lauda	Ferrari 312B3
53	French GP	*Dijon-Prenois*	7 July 1974	Ronnie Peterson	Lotus 72E-Ford
54	British GP	*Brands Hatch*	20 July 1974	Jody Scheckter	Tyrrell 007-Ford
55	German GP	*Nürburgring*	4 August 1974	Clay Regazzoni	Ferrari 312B3
56	Austrian GP	*Österreichring*	18 August 1974	Carlos Reutemann	Brabham BT44-Ford
57	Italian GP	*Monza*	8 September 1974	Ronnie Peterson	Lotus 72E-Ford
58	Canadian GP	*Mosport Park*	22 September 1974	Emerson Fittipaldi	McLaren M23-Ford
59	US GP	*Watkins Glen*	6 October 1974	Carlos Reutemann	Brabham BT44-Ford
60	Argentine GP	*Buenos Aires*	12 January 1975	Emerson Fittipaldi	McLaren M23-Ford
61	Brazilian GP	*Interlagos*	26 January 1975	Carlos Pace	Brabham BT44B-Ford
62	South African GP	*Kyalami*	1 March 1975	Jody Scheckter	Tyrrell 007-Ford
63	Spanish GP	*Montjuich Park*	27 April 1975	Jochen Mass	McLaren M23-Ford
64	Monaco GP	*Monte Carlo*	11 May 1975	Niki Lauda	Ferrari 312T
65	Belgian GP	*Zolder*	25 May 1975	Niki Lauda	Ferrari 312T
66	Swedish GP	*Anderstorp*	8 June 1975	Niki Lauda	Ferrari 312T
67	Dutch GP	*Zandvoort*	22 June 1975	James Hunt	Hesketh 308-Ford
68	French GP	*Paul Ricard*	6 July 1975	Niki Lauda	Ferrari 312T
69	British GP	*Silverstone*	19 July 1975	Emerson Fittipaldi	McLaren M23-Ford
70	German GP	*Nürburgring*	3 August 1975	Carlos Reutemann	Brabham BT44B-Ford
71	Austrian GP	*Österreichring*	17 August 1975	Vittorio Brambilla	March 751-Ford
72	Italian GP	*Monza*	7 September 1975	Clay Regazzoni	Ferrari 312T
73	US GP	*Watkins Glen*	5 October 1975	Niki Lauda	Ferrari 312T
74	Brazilian GP	*Interlagos*	25 January 1976	Niki Lauda	Ferrari 312T
75	South African GP	*Kyalami*	6 March 1976	Niki Lauda	Ferrari 312T
76	US GP West	*Long Beach*	28 March 1976	Clay Regazzoni	Ferrari 312T
77	Spanish GP	*Jarama*	2 May 1976	James Hunt	McLaren M23-Ford
78	Belgian GP	*Zolder*	16 May 1976	Niki Lauda	Ferrari 312T2
79	Monaco GP	*Monte Carlo*	30 May 1976	Niki Lauda	Ferrari 312T2
80	Swedish GP	*Anderstorp*	13 June 1976	Jody Scheckter	Tyrrell P34-Ford
81	French GP	*Paul Ricard*	4 July 1976	James Hunt	McLaren M23-Ford
82	British GP	*Brands Hatch*	18 July 1976	Niki Lauda	Ferrari 312T2
83	German GP	*Nürburgring*	1 August 1976	James Hunt	McLaren M23-Ford
84	Austrian GP	*Österreichring*	15 August 1976	John Watson	Penske PC4-Ford
85	Dutch GP	*Zandvoort*	29 August 1976	James Hunt	McLaren M23-Ford
86	Italian GP	*Monza*	12 September 1976	Ronnie Peterson	March 761-Ford
87	Canadian GP	*Mosport Park*	3 October 1976	James Hunt	McLaren M23-Ford
88	US GP	*Watkins Glen*	10 October 1976	James Hunt	McLaren M23-Ford
89	Japanese GP	*Fuji*	24 October 1976	Mario Andretti	Lotus 77-Ford
90	Argentine GP	*Buenos Aires*	9 January 1977	Jody Scheckter	Wolf WR1-Ford
91	Brazilian GP	*Interlagos*	23 January 1977	Carlos Reutemann	Ferrari 312T2
92	South African GP	*Kyalami*	5 March 1977	Niki Lauda	Ferrari 312T2
93	US GP West	*Long Beach*	3 April 1977	Mario Andretti	Lotus 78-Ford
94	Spanish GP	*Jarama*	8 May 1977	Mario Andretti	Lotus 78-Ford
95	Monaco GP	*Monte Carlo*	22 May 1977	Jody Scheckter	Wolf WR1-Ford
96	Belgian GP	*Zolder*	5 June 1977	Gunnar Nilsson	Lotus 78-Ford
97	Swedish GP	*Anderstorp*	19 June 1977	Jacques Laffite	Ligier JS7-Matra
98	French GP	*Dijon-Prenois*	3 July 1977	Mario Andretti	Lotus 78-Ford
99	British GP	*Silverstone*	16 July 1977	James Hunt	McLaren M26-Ford
100	German GP	*Hockenheim*	31 July 1977	Niki Lauda	Ferrari 312T2

	EVENT	VENUE	DATE	DRIVER	CAR
101	Austrian GP	*Österreichring*	14 August 1977	Alan Jones	Shadow DN8A-Ford
102	Dutch GP	*Zandvoort*	28 August 1977	Niki Lauda	Ferrari 312T2
103	Italian GP	*Monza*	11 September 1977	Mario Andretti	Lotus 78-Ford
104	US GP	*Watkins Glen*	2 October 1977	James Hunt	McLaren M26-Ford
105	Canadian GP	*Mosport Park*	9 October 1977	Jody Scheckter	Wolf WR1-Ford
106	Japanese GP	*Fuji*	23 October 1977	James Hunt	McLaren M26-Ford
107	Argentine GP	*Buenos Aires*	15 January 1978	Mario Andretti	Lotus 78-Ford
108	South African GP	*Kyalami*	4 March 1978	Ronnie Peterson	Lotus 78-Ford
109	Monaco GP	*Monte Carlo*	7 May 1978	Patrick Depailler	Tyrrell 008-Ford
110	Belgian GP	*Zolder*	21 May 1978	Mario Andretti	Lotus 79-Ford
111	Spanish GP	*Jarama*	4 June 1978	Mario Andretti	Lotus 79-Ford
112	Swedish GP	*Anderstorp*	17 June 1978	Niki Lauda	Brabham BT46-Alfa Romeo
113	French GP	*Paul Ricard*	2 July 1978	Mario Andretti	Lotus 79-Ford
114	German GP	*Hockenheim*	30 July 1978	Mario Andretti	Lotus 79-Ford
115	Austrian GP	*Österreichring*	13 August 1978	Ronnie Peterson	Lotus 79-Ford
116	Dutch GP	*Zandvoort*	27 August 1978	Mario Andretti	Lotus 79-Ford
117	Italian GP	*Monza*	10 September 1978	Niki Lauda	Brabham BT46-Alfa Romeo
118	Argentine GP	*Buenos Aires*	21 January 1979	Jacques Laffite	Ligier JS11-Ford
119	Brazilian GP	*Interlagos*	4 February 1979	Jacques Laffite	Ligier JS11-Ford
120	Spanish GP	*Jarama*	29 April 1979	Patrick Depailler	Ligier JS11-Ford
121	British GP	*Silverstone*	14 July 1979	Clay Regazzoni	Williams FW07-Ford
122	German GP	*Hockenheim*	29 July 1979	Alan Jones	Williams FW07-Ford
123	Austrian GP	*Österreichring*	12 August 1979	Alan Jones	Williams FW07-Ford
124	Dutch GP	*Zandvoort*	26 August 1979	Alan Jones	Williams FW07-Ford
125	Canadian GP	*Montreal*	30 September 1979	Alan Jones	Williams FW07-Ford
126	Argentine GP	*Buenos Aires*	13 January 1980	Alan Jones	Williams FW07-Ford
127	US GP West	*Long Beach*	30 March 1980	Nelson Piquet	Brabham BT49-Ford
128	Belgian GP	*Zolder*	4 May 1980	Didier Pironi	Ligier JS11/15-Ford
129	Monaco GP	*Monte Carlo*	18 May 1980	Carlos Reutemann	Williams FW07B-Ford
130	French GP	*Paul Ricard*	29 June 1980	Alan Jones	Williams FW07B-Ford
131	British GP	*Brands Hatch*	13 July 1980	Alan Jones	Williams FW07B-Ford
132	German GP	*Hockenheim*	10 August 1980	Jacques Laffite	Ligier JS11/15-Ford
133	Dutch GP	*Zandvoort*	31 August 1980	Nelson Piquet	Brabham BT49-Ford
134	Italian GP	*Imola*	14 September 1980	Nelson Piquet	Brabham BT49-Ford
135	Canadian GP	*Montreal*	28 September 1980	Alan Jones	Williams FW07B-Ford
136	US GP	*Watkins Glen*	5 October 1980	Alan Jones	Williams FW07B-Ford
137	German GP	*Hockenheim*	2 August 1981	Nelson Piquet	Brabham BT49C-Ford
138	Caesar's Palace GP	*Las Vegas*	17 October 1981	Alan Jones	Williams FW07B-Ford
139	San Marino GP	*Imola*	25 April 1982	Didier Pironi	Ferrari 126C2
140	Monaco GP	*Monte Carlo*	23 May 1982	Riccardo Patrese	Brabham BT49D-Ford
141	Canadian GP	*Montreal*	13 June 1982	Nelson Piquet	Brabham BT50-BMW
142	Dutch GP	*Zandvoort*	3 July 1982	Didier Pironi	Ferrari 126C2
143	German GP	*Hockenheim*	8 August 1982	Patrick Tambay	Ferrari 126C2
144	Austrian GP	*Österreichring*	15 August 1982	Elio de Angelis	Lotus 91-Ford
145	Swiss GP	*Dijon-Prenois*	29 August 1982	Keke Rosberg	Williams FW08-Ford
146	Caesar's Palace GP	*Las Vegas*	25 September 1982	Michele Alboreto	Tyrrell 011-Ford
147	San Marino GP	*Imola*	1 May 1983	Patrick Tambay	Ferrari 126C2B
148	Monaco GP	*Monte Carlo*	15 May 1983	Keke Rosberg	Williams FW08C-Ford
149	US GP	*Detroit*	5 June 1983	Michele Alboreto	Tyrrell 011-Ford
150	Canadian GP	*Montreal*	12 June 1983	René Arnoux	Ferrari 126C2B

	EVENT	VENUE	DATE	DRIVER	CAR
151	German GP	*Hockenheim*	7 August 1983	René Arnoux	Ferrari 126C3
152	Dutch GP	*Zandvoort*	28 August 1983	René Arnoux	Ferrari 126C3
153	Belgian GP	*Zolder*	29 April 1984	Michele Alboreto	Ferrari 126C4
154	Dallas GP	*Fair Park*	8 July 1984	Keke Rosberg	Williams FW09-Honda
155	Brazilian GP	*Jacarepaguá*	7 April 1985	Alain Prost	McLaren MP4/2B-Porsche
156	Portuguese GP	*Estoril*	21 April 1985	Ayrton Senna	Lotus 97T-Renault
157	San Marino GP	*Imola*	5 May 1985	Elio de Angelis	Lotus 97T-Renault
158	Monaco GP	*Monte Carlo*	19 May 1985	Alain Prost	McLaren MP4/2B-Porsche
159	Canadian GP	*Montreal*	16 June 1985	Michele Alboreto	Ferrari 156/85
160	US GP	*Detroit*	23 June 1985	Keke Rosberg	Williams FW10-Honda
161	British GP	*Silverstone*	21 July 1985	Alain Prost	McLaren MP4/2B-Porsche
162	German GP	*New Nürburgring*	4 August 1985	Michele Alboreto	Ferrari 156/85
163	Austrian GP	*Österreichring*	18 August 1985	Alain Prost	McLaren MP4/2B-Porsche
164	Dutch GP	*Zandvoort*	25 August 1985	Niki Lauda	McLaren MP4/2B-Porsche
165	Italian GP	*Monza*	8 September 1985	Alain Prost	McLaren MP4/2B-Porsche
166	Belgian GP	*Spa-Francorchamps*	15 September 1985	Ayrton Senna	Lotus 97T-Renault
167	European GP	*Brands Hatch*	6 October 1985	Nigel Mansell	Williams FW10-Honda
168	South African GP	*Kyalami*	19 October 1985	Nigel Mansell	Williams FW10-Honda
169	Australian GP	*Adelaide*	3 November 1985	Keke Rosberg	Williams FW10-Honda
170	Brazilian GP	*Jacarepaguá*	23 March 1986	Nelson Piquet	Williams FW11-Honda
171	Spanish GP	*Jerez*	13 April 1986	Ayrton Senna	Lotus 98T-Renault
172	San Marino GP	*Imola*	27 April 1986	Alain Prost	McLaren MP4/2C-Porsche
173	Monaco GP	*Monte Carlo*	11 May 1986	Alain Prost	McLaren MP4/2C-Porsche
174	Belgian GP	*Spa-Francorchamps*	25 May 1986	Nigel Mansell	Williams FW11-Honda
175	Canadian GP	*Montreal*	15 June 1986	Nigel Mansell	Williams FW11-Honda
176	US GP	*Detroit*	22 June 1986	Ayrton Senna	Lotus 98T-Renault
177	French GP	*Paul Ricard*	6 July 1986	Nigel Mansell	Williams FW11-Honda
178	British GP	*Brands Hatch*	13 July 1986	Nigel Mansell	Williams FW11-Honda
179	German GP	*Hockenheim*	27 July 1986	Nelson Piquet	Williams FW11-Honda
180	Hungarian GP	*Hungaroring*	10 August 1986	Nelson Piquet	Williams FW11-Honda
181	Austrian GP	*Österreichring*	17 August 1986	Alain Prost	McLaren MP4/2C-Porsche
182	Italian GP	*Monza*	7 September 1986	Nelson Piquet	Williams FW11-Honda
183	Portuguese GP	*Estoril*	21 September 1986	Nigel Mansell	Williams FW11-Honda
184	Australian GP	*Adelaide*	26 October 1986	Alain Prost	McLaren MP4/2C-Porsche
185	Brazilian GP	*Jacarepaguá*	12 April 1987	Alain Prost	McLaren MP4/3-Porsche
186	San Marino GP	*Imola*	3 May 1987	Nigel Mansell	Williams FW11B-Honda
187	Belgian GP	*Spa-Francorchamps*	17 May 1987	Alain Prost	McLaren MP4/3-Porsche
188	Monaco GP	*Monte Carlo*	31 May 1987	Ayrton Senna	Lotus 99T-Honda
189	US GP	*Detroit*	21 June 1987	Ayrton Senna	Lotus 99T-Honda
190	French GP	*Paul Ricard*	5 July 1987	Nigel Mansell	Williams FW11B-Honda
191	British GP	*Silverstone*	12 July 1987	Nigel Mansell	Williams FW11B-Honda
192	German GP	*Hockenheim*	26 July 1987	Nelson Piquet	Williams FW11B-Honda
193	Hungarian GP	*Hungaroring*	9 August 1987	Nelson Piquet	Williams FW11B-Honda
194	Austrian GP	*Österreichring*	16 August 1987	Nigel Mansell	Williams FW11B-Honda
195	Italian GP	*Monza*	6 September 1987	Nelson Piquet	Williams FW11B-Honda
196	Portuguese GP	*Estoril*	20 September 1987	Alain Prost	McLaren MP4/3-Porsche
197	Spanish GP	*Jerez*	27 September 1987	Nigel Mansell	Williams FW11B-Honda
198	Mexican GP	*Mexico City*	18 October 1987	Nigel Mansell	Williams FW11B-Honda
199	Japanese GP	*Suzuka*	1 November 1987	Gerhard Berger	Ferrari F1/87
200	Australian GP	*Adelaide*	15 November 1987	Gerhard Berger	Ferrari F1/87

	EVENT	VENUE	DATE	DRIVER	CAR
201	Brazilian GP	*Jacarepaguá*	3 April 1988	Alain Prost	McLaren MP4/4-Honda
202	San Marino GP	*Imola*	1 May 1988	Ayrton Senna	McLaren MP4/4-Honda
203	Monaco GP	*Monte Carlo*	15 May 1988	Alain Prost	McLaren MP4/4-Honda
204	Mexican GP	*Mexico City*	29 May 1988	Alain Prost	McLaren MP4/4-Honda
205	Canadian GP	*Montreal*	12 June 1988	Ayrton Senna	McLaren MP4/4-Honda
206	US GP	*Detroit*	19 June 1988	Ayrton Senna	McLaren MP4/4-Honda
207	French GP	*Paul Ricard*	3 July 1988	Alain Prost	McLaren MP4/4-Honda
208	British GP	*Silverstone*	10 July 1988	Ayrton Senna	McLaren MP4/4-Honda
209	German GP	*Hockenheim*	24 July 1988	Ayrton Senna	McLaren MP4/4-Honda
210	Hungarian GP	*Hungaroring*	7 August 1988	Ayrton Senna	McLaren MP4/4-Honda
211	Belgian GP	*Spa-Francorchamps*	28 August 1988	Ayrton Senna	McLaren MP4/4-Honda
212	Italian GP	*Monza*	11 September 1988	Gerhard Berger	Ferrari F1/87/88C
213	Portuguese GP	*Estoril*	25 September 1988	Alain Prost	McLaren MP4/4-Honda
214	Spanish GP	*Jerez*	2 October 1988	Alain Prost	McLaren MP4/4-Honda
215	Japanese GP	*Suzuka*	30 October 1988	Ayrton Senna	McLaren MP4/4-Honda
216	Australian GP	*Adelaide*	13 November 1988	Alain Prost	McLaren MP4/4-Honda
217	Brazilian GP	*Jacarepaguá*	26 March 1989	Nigel Mansell	Ferrari 640
218	San Marino GP	*Imola*	23 April 1989	Ayrton Senna	McLaren MP4/5-Honda
219	Monaco GP	*Monte Carlo*	7 May 1989	Ayrton Senna	McLaren MP4/5-Honda
220	Mexican GP	*Mexico City*	28 May 1989	Ayrton Senna	McLaren MP4/5-Honda
221	US GP	*Phoenix*	4 June 1989	Alain Prost	McLaren MP4/5-Honda
222	Canadian GP	*Montreal*	18 June 1989	Thierry Boutsen	Williams FW12C-Renault
223	French GP	*Paul Ricard*	9 July 1989	Alain Prost	McLaren MP4/5-Honda
224	British GP	*Silverstone*	16 July 1989	Alain Prost	McLaren MP4/5-Honda
225	German GP	*Hockenheim*	30 July 1989	Ayrton Senna	McLaren MP4/5-Honda
226	Hungarian GP	*Hungaroring*	13 August 1989	Nigel Mansell	Ferrari 640
227	Belgian GP	*Spa-Francorchamps*	27 August 1989	Ayrton Senna	McLaren MP4/5-Honda
228	Italian GP	*Monza*	10 September 1989	Alain Prost	McLaren MP4/5-Honda
229	Portuguese GP	*Estoril*	24 September 1989	Gerhard Berger	Ferrari 640
230	Spanish GP	*Jerez*	1 October 1989	Ayrton Senna	McLaren MP4/5-Honda
231	Japanese GP	*Suzuka*	22 October 1989	Alessandro Nannini	Benetton B189-Ford
232	Australian GP	*Adelaide*	5 November 1989	Thierry Boutsen	Williams FW13-Renault
233	US GP	*Phoenix*	11 March 1990	Ayrton Senna	McLaren MP4/5B-Honda
234	Brazilian GP	*Interlagos*	25 March 1990	Alain Prost	Ferrari 641
235	San Marino GP	*Imola*	13 May 1990	Riccardo Patrese	Williams FW13B-Renault
236	Monaco GP	*Monte Carlo*	27 May 1990	Ayrton Senna	McLaren MP4/5B-Honda
237	Canadian GP	*Montreal*	10 June 1990	Ayrton Senna	McLaren MP4/5B-Honda
238	Mexican GP	*Mexico City*	24 June 1990	Alain Prost	Ferrari 641
239	French GP	*Paul Ricard*	8 July 1990	Alain Prost	Ferrari 641
240	British GP	*Silverstone*	15 July 1990	Alain Prost	Ferrari 641
241	German GP	*Hockenheim*	29 July 1990	Ayrton Senna	McLaren MP4/5B-Honda
242	Hungarian GP	*Hungaroring*	12 August 1990	Thierry Boutsen	Williams FW13B-Renault
243	Belgian GP	*Spa-Francorchamps*	26 August 1990	Ayrton Senna	McLaren MP4/5B-Honda
244	Italian GP	*Monza*	9 September 1990	Ayrton Senna	McLaren MP4/5B-Honda
245	Portuguese GP	*Estoril*	23 September 1990	Nigel Mansell	Ferrari 641
246	Spanish GP	*Jerez*	30 September 1990	Alain Prost	Ferrari 641
247	Japanese GP	*Suzuka*	21 October 1990	Nelson Piquet	Benetton B190-Ford
248	Australian GP	*Adelaide*	4 November 1990	Nelson Piquet	Benetton B190-Ford
249	US GP	*Phoenix*	10 March 1991	Ayrton Senna	McLaren MP4/6-Honda
250	Brazilian GP	*Interlagos*	24 March 1991	Ayrton Senna	McLaren MP4/6-Honda

GOODYEAR
GOODYEAR
Racing